AN IRISH EYE

Also by Anthony Cronin

Poetry

Poems
Collected Poems
Reductionist Poem
41 Sonnet-Poems 82
New and Selected Poems

Prose

Dead as Doornails
The Life of Riley
Identity Papers
A Question of Modernity
Heritage Now: Irish Literature in the English Language

Drama

The Shame Of It

An Irish Eye

Anthony Cronin

BRANDON

First published 1985
Brandon Book Publishers Ltd.,
Dingle, Co. Kerry;
and 51 Washington Street,
Dover, New Hampshire 03820, U.S.A.

© Anthony Cronin 1985

This book is published with the financial assistance of the Arts Council/*An Chomhairle Ealaíon,* Ireland.

Typesetting & make-up: Vermilion
Printed by: Mount Salus Press, Dublin, Ireland.

To
*all those among my fellow artists
who consider such topics
worthy of discussion*

Author's Note

All but one of these pieces were first published as "Viewpoint" columns in THE IRISH TIMES. They are not fully representative of the subjects treated in the column, however. Ireland, as it is now and as it came to be so, is the binding theme here; even if some of the more philosophical pieces are relevant to other places as well.

I have made few alterations and then only in the interests of clarity. A journalist flinging his thoughts together in haste is more liable to error than many; but I have not chased up every fact and quotation anew. My subject, as often as not, is history; let my errors, of fact or interpretation, be history too.

Since Brian Fallon edited the page on which the original column appeared, I would like to make grateful acknowledgement here of his respect for his contributor's independence. The odd piece out, "England on a Clear Day", was a preface to the catalogue of "A Sense of Ireland".

Anthony Cronin
London
August 1984

Contents

The Bould Robert Emmet.............................9
Loud Huzzas 14
The Chief Again 17
Dev Contra Mundum 22
The Failure of Jim Larkin.........................27
Farewell Kiltartan................................32
The Cradle of the Race............................37
What You Voted For................................41
The Easy Years....................................45
West of Clondalkin................................48
Who's for Culture?................................52
Material and Spiritual............................55
God and Mammon....................................58
Some More Equal Than Others.......................61
Public Enterprise.................................65
Larning or Larupping?.............................68
A Time to Rejoice In..............................71
What Next?..74

Stasis Under The Crown 77
The Famous Declaration 82
H-Block 88
Pomp and Circumstance 92
Till The Boys Come Home 96
The Brotherhood of Man 99
Liberation All Round 103
Onward, Sisters, Onward 107
Kept in Idleness 111
Time On Our Hands 115
The Hard Facts 118
The Republican Dilemma 123
Up The Republic! 127
Save Ye Kindly Ma'am 132
England On A Clear Day 136

The Bould Robert Emmet

THERE ISN'T going to be much fuss about the bi-centenary of the birth of Robert Emmet; and the reasons are not far to seek. Republicanism, nationalism, separatism of all sorts, shades and descriptions, are, in spite of the Giant Electoral Victory of the Republican Party, still at a pretty low ebb. Heroism, pure and undefiled, at a low rate of discount; romanticism, shining and bright, at an even lower; martyrdom, a joke in poor taste: and a hero, a martyr who died with a smile is, as we all know too well, what the bould Robert Emmet is supposed to have been.

But he was also a revolutionary conspirator; and even supposing such people were approved of in these parts nowadays — which they most certainly are not — he would not be regarded as any sort of advertisement for the breed. For Emmet, in that department, was the arch bungler. The figure he presents to the world is one of quite astonishing ineptitude and carelessness. The fate of Lord Kilwarden, the "remarkably humane" Lord Chief Justice whom "the mob" (aided by the seldom-referred-to agents provocateurs) pulled from his carriage and piked in the street rivals his own in its fame.

The cruelly dismissive chapter in Mr Robert Kee's widely circulated "The Green Flag" just about sums up the current attitudes, as doubtless it is meant to, for my old friend Mr Kee's work is, sad to say, a deliberate job of de-bunking right through; and as such it is, on the whole, just about as a-historical as the old bunking jobs on which we were brought up. Mr Kee insists that as the would-be head of a revolutionary mass movement, Emmet was a presumptious, elitist bore, ready to drag a cowed and anxious people into a calamity of his own creating; while as a conspirator, with his drunken messengers, his premature explosions, his mixed-up fuses, his bolting cab-horses and his signal rockets that were never fired, he cuts a totally ridiculous figure.

It is a far, far cry from the days when he hung in his green cut-away coat and white pantaloons on every cottage wall. In spite of Mr George Colley's visit to Kilmainham, Emmet, in the popular estimation nowadays, was a bit of an eejit, and the less said about him the better.

Interestingly enough, all the efforts of the Administration at the time were directed towards making Emmet a ridiculous figure with elitist notions also. He had in the words Norbury used in the candle-lit courtroom, "the honour to be a gentleman by birth" whose father "filled a respectable situation" under the Crown; but, the prisoner was told, "you have conspired with hostlers, bakers, butchers, and such persons, whom you invited to council when you erected your provisional government." The prosecuting lawyer could barely contain his amusement at the contrast in social station between Emmet and his associates, Dowdall the clerk, Quigley the bricklayer, Stafford the baker, " illiterate victims of the ambition of this young man." In all the Administration's unctuous pronouncements, in the editorials of its bought newspapers and the orations of its doubtless more-easily-convinced lawyers, the point is hammered home. Emmet was a dilettante and his followers were "miserable victims" who had been "misled by phantoms of revolutionary delusion."

At the same time, of course, there had to have been horrors committed and further horrors untold in the prospect of success. The young gentleman from Trinity College, Mr William Conyngham Plunket told the jury, "would doubtless have been immolated by his followers if he had succeeded." A Jacobin terror was a clear possibility, as the fate of Lord Kilwarden should remind everybody. And when it was all over the *Dublin Evening Post* (whose editor, incidentally, was drawing a secret service allowance of one hundred pounds a quarter) hammered the points thus far made home. Emmet's associates were "an outlawed bricklayer, and such contemptible creatures, as an outlawed clerk, hodmen, hostlers, old clothes men, etc."

The conspiracy therefore "was contemptible and inefficient, and stood isolated and detached from popular sympathy and co-operation." Yet at the same time "it was one of those efforts of mob-like riot and licentiousness to which mad enthusiasm can almost at any time, with the aid of a little money, rouse the desperate profligacy of a great capital."

In other words, the prosecution's case was much the same as Mr Kee's; the only difference being the unspoken admission, reflecting an unspoken fear, that Emmet had nearly succeeded in getting out of the web of conspiracy and making himself the leader of a mass movement which included a very large number of honest working-class people. But being the same as Mr Kee's, it is the same as the general opinion which Mr Kee has helped to form: Emmet was the creator of unecessary bloodshed, brutal, inefficient and hopeless all at the same time, and as such little better than a murderer.

And opposed to this stupid, sordid and unnecessary invocation of violence, with its degrading means and its impossible object, stood, according to Mr Conyngham Plunkett, the ordinary processes of politics and the law:

> What does it avow itself to be? A plan – not to correct the excesses or reform the abuses of the government of the country; not to remove any specks of imperfection which might have grown upon the surface of this constitution, or to restrain the overgrown power of the Crown, or to restore any privilege of parliament, or to throw any new security round the liberty of the subject. No. But it plainly and boldly avows itself to be a plan to separate Great Britain from Ireland; to dissolve the Union and put "a free and independent republic in Ireland" in its place. To sever the connection between Great Britain and Ireland!
>
> Gentlemen, I should feel it a waste of words and public time were I addressing you or any person within the limits of my voice to talk of the frantic desperation of the plan of any man, who speculates upon the dissolution of that empire, whose glory and happiness depend upon its indissoluble connection. But were it practicable to sever that connection, to untie the links that bind us to the British constitution, and to turn us adrift upon the turbulent ocean of revolution, who could answer for the existence of this country, as an independent power, for a year? God and nature have made the two countries essential to each other. Let them cling to each other. Let them cling to each other to the end of time, and their united affection and loyalty will be proof against the machinations of the world.

Mr Plunkett, of course, could not see into the future. The Act of Union was only three years old; and he could no more at that stage have foreseen the cynical lack of any attempt to make it work as it was supposed to work than he could have prognosticated the "glory and happiness" of the death-toll which the system under which Ireland then laboured was to bring about four decades later. Nor, we may be mildly assured, did Mr Plunkett much care. He had spoken, in company with the egregiously obnoxious Curran and Tom Emmet's old friend the part-time informer Peter Burrowes, against the Union, and he was at this moment most anxious to work his passage home. But nothing in the records of the time is more striking than the contrast between the idealism of Robert Emmet and the self-seeking, the brief-hunting, the placemanship, the cool run-of-the-mill chicanery and corruption of everybody who surrounded him with the exception of his own hostlers, butchers and brickmakers.

It may be said – as indeed the prosecution and the propagandists said in effect – that Emmet's "idealism" was merely the sublimation and the guise of a different kind of ambition, which might have included martyrdom but nevertheless involved the ruin and death of a great many other people. We know a good deal now, we think, about the psychology of heroism, and perhaps of romanticism also, which is not to its credit. But nevertheless the contrast remains, and in viewing the picture – the smooth-talking, bought lawyers with their assurances that the law had the answer to every complaint, the careerist politicians with their reasonable belief in progress, the dissolute editors with their clever echoes of the middle-class man in the street, the enormous network of spies and secret agents with their eye to the main chance on one side; and the youthful, pathetic figure with its pleading voice and its belief in human idealism on the other – a lot will depend on the respondent's most instinctual and fundamental reactions.

Yet again, we would be falling into a trap carefully enough set in most times and places if we allow ourselves to be on the side of mere "idealism". For in what way, we should really ask ourselves, were Emmet's ideas less worthy of respect than his opponents'? The thirty decrees attached to the Proclamation of the Provisional Government which was read by the light of smoky candles to the hostlers and hod-carriers in the depot in Thomas Street (and met with their approval) abolished tithes; made Church lands the property of the nation; suspended all dealings in land and securities until the formation of a national government; and instituted a sovereign assembly elected by universal suffrage and secret ballot.

The Proclamation itself declared that: "We war not against property, we war against no religious sect, we war not against past opinions or prejudices, we war against English dominion." Not very original-sounding now, perhaps, and if impracticable only because it was, as they say, "far in advance of its time." But the validity of Emmet's ideas was and is somehow held to be affected by the fact that he was still sending out to buy blunderbusses a few minutes before he led out his pikemen; while the practicality of his opponents' was amply endorsed when, the day after his trial, the banker Luke White called at the Castle and said he would immediately take £500,000 in Exchequer-bills at par.

But the final and most cruel of all the ironies contained in Emmet's and Ireland's situation is perhaps revealed by a clearer look at his actual character and abilities than the romanticism of subsequent generations, the sordidity of his failure and the subtle calumnies of his opponents have perhaps ever permitted. He was only twenty-four years of age when he returned from Paris, reaffirmed his connection with the United Irishmen and entered on his disastrous, conspiratorial course. A year later his charm, ability and attractions (including, of course, his class-attractions) had placed him at the head of what in hard fact did very nearly become a mass movement of daunting proportions, with a fair chance of success.

There are questions still unanswered about its failure; but the ability and the eloquence of the boy leader are surely undeniable.

He made his famous speech from the dock unrefreshed, late at night and in the face of hostile and effective interruption, after standing in the courtroom for more than twelve hours. If Ireland had been a free country, or Irish society had been a free society in which a man of honour could have cared to rise, there is absolutely no doubt whatever that Emmet would have distinguished himself as a politician of humane instincts and near-to-dazzling genius. But the situation in which his country found itself forced him, as it has done so many others, to turn his talents in a particular direction for which he was totally unfitted. He was perhaps the most inept conspirator on record; and on that alone, he is apparently, by current consensus, to be judged.

Loud Huzzas

AS FAR as the majority of the Irish people were concerned, Catholic Emancipation was one of the great non-events in a country whose history has been a curious alternation between non-event and real calamity. Most of the penal laws had been repealed in the 1780's and 1790's; and before ever O'Connell began his agitation Catholics had freedom of worship and of religious education. Those who were lucky enough to acquire it could hold any sort of property and make any use of it that the law permitted anybody else; and the members of the Catholic middle class and upper class could freely enter and practise the professions.

They could not, it is true, be captains in His Majesty's navy, nor colonels in his army, nor could they in general be anything but subordinates in the civil service as it was then; but to most of the inhabitants of Clare and elsewhere the possibility of becoming any of these things was, to say the least, remote. As is so often the case when the generality are aroused by an emotive dream of an old order ending, the real irritant was one which affected only an ambitious few: Catholics could neither be members of Parliament nor of the Inner Bar.

Of course to say that it did not matter to the vast majority of the population who allegedly represented them, or the voters amongst them in Parliament, would be to raise large questions about representation in general; while about representation in the Westminster Parliament in the third decade of the nineteenth century and its precise value the experts are probably best left to have their say. But even a non-expert can safely hazard that the actual results of Emancipation in this respect were woefully and ludicrously out of proportion to the hazy expectations of the unwashed multitude.

After "Emancipation" the Liberator led a small band of Irish members in the House of Commons who wrung occasional concessions from the indolent Whig aristos in return for occasional support; and in the twelve years before the defeat of the Liberal Party and the return of Sir Robert Peel's Tory squires and supercillious noblemen (at which time O'Connell's influence came to an end and he became a convert to Repeal) they secured a slight increase in Irish representation, an equivalent for Ireland of the English measures concerning the reorganisation of municipal government and a partial abolition of tithes. Most of this would have come anyway in the climate of reform which had been inaugurated not by Emancipation, but by the original victory of the Whigs and their merchant allies — as indeed Emancipation itself would surely have come.

The parallels with many aspects of the power-sharing struggle in the north-eastern part of Ireland will be obvious. A political irritant had been removed. The more ambitious, the more purely politically-minded had been enabled to begin to integrate themselves into the machinery of politics (or, if you like, into the democratic process). A victory for "us" over "them" had been given institutional reality. A few reforms (which might have come anyway) had been effected. And in the meantime Ireland continued towards the ultimate disaster of the Famine, with all the sterner questions un-asked and all the real problems utterly untouched. It would in fact need an extreme ironist, and perhaps one who actually rejoiced in humanity's idiocy such as Jonathan Swift, to do justice to the contrast between the extraordinary upsurge of emotion and expectation, between the men of Feakle and Scarriff marching into Ennis behind their priests with their green boughs and their shamrocks wreathed in gold, and the poor reality that victory represented.

In so far as Emancipation was a real victory at all, it was a victory for a class or a section of a class. The upper echelons of the Catholic middle classes had gained something and the lawyers among them had gained most. The type of jolly, well-fed, Jesuit-educated lawyer in politics with which we are still so familiar had been put on a par with his Protestant counterpart and would never look back. A few learned MacPangloss's, products of Clongowes and other establishments, could now put KC after their names, double their fees and look forward perhaps to Judgeships.

But in this respect at least, whatever about others, O'Connell himself was to be disappointed. The senile George IV, still defying the earlier sins of the "first gentleman" to carry off the anointed king, lasted long enough to refuse him the special patent which was never afterwards granted. Charles Butler, the eighty-year-old secretary to the English Catholics, whose loyalty to the crown was so great that he had actually agitated in favour of the Veto, was chosen to be the first Catholic KC; a bevy of Dublin lawyers was also promoted; and while Dan was passed over, Sheil was chosen, Sheil who, as Denis Gwynn says, "had been only a boy while O'Connell was rousing the country when Peel first came to Dublin as a very young man; who had disappeared from the agitation for years, and had only come to prominence again when O'Connell persuaded him to become his ally in forming the Catholic association." The following year the Liberator more or less abandoned the practice of his ungrateful profession, giving up eight thousand pounds a year at the bar in favour of thirteen thousand pounds per annum as the people's representative. But if he never, as he put it himself, "obtained the precedency of a silk gown," at least a youthful dream of becoming a member of Parliament came true.

To be fair to O'Connell he knew very well that; "although the Catholic aristocracy and gentry of Ireland had obtained the most valuable advantages from Emancipation, yet the benefit of good government had not reached the great mass of the Irish people, and could not reach them unless the Union should be made a reality or unless the hideous measure should be abrogated." Emancipation was a prelude to nothing and in its extreme way it was therefore typical of all political movements, whether monarchist, nationalist, republican, racist, religious or anything else, which are not rooted in social reality or which cannot be seen to be a prelude to and a clearing of the way for social realities. In its emotion-filled worthlessness it set a very bad precedent for political arousal in Ireland. The Claremen had their day at the hustings; and of course also there was a little walking tall, a little restoration of dignity and a little affirmation of equality. The same results can be, and are, produced every day by football matches.

And the cost was terrible. Emancipation as an issue was utterly remote from Ireland's chaotic systems of land tenure and the futile methods of agriculture which they bred. When De Tocqueville came to Ireland in 1835, in spite of great human virtues, he saw nothing but misery. Starvation was endemic, but he noted also the desperation of as many members of the debt-ridden aristocracy as were to be encountered. Burdened as usual by chimeras of all descriptions, Ireland plunged on towards the Famine and its aftermath. This was not (needless to say) in any way the result of Catholic Emancipation, nor was it Daniel O'Connell's fault. But the foolish diversion of energy, the clouding of clear vision and all that went with them were in part at least his fault. And the great man was also a great corrupter. The type of politics which he initiated — Tammany, priest-regarding, keeping a tight grip on each locality but choosing always the issue of immediate advantage to the politician — has been with us to this day. It is arguable that it has done as much damage as the tradition of violence that is now so universally held in detestation.

The Chief Again

IT IS not so long since political biographers discovered politics, and the effect has been almost equivalent to Lytton Strachey's discovery that a certain degree of eminence could be combined with a partiality for brandy and soda or with homosexual tendencies. To the political biographers of a former age the important thing was the "aim in life", the "destiny" or the "mission". They would admit — as Morley admitted in the case of Gladstone — that a certain amount of political double-think was necessary if their particular great man was to achieve great political ends, but they minimised it and their general tendency was to regret the necessity rather than to glorify the skill involved.

Then came the discovery that in politics, politics are important; and it went to the biographers' heads.

Just as in post-Strachey biography the feet of clay became the focus of attention to the practical exclusion of the face of granite, so the dominant theme of political biography became the wheelings and dealings, the manoeuvrings and the deceptions themselves.

An amusing instance of this occurs on page 445 of Dr F.S.L. Lyons's biography of Parnell. In 1889, when the flowing tide was at its fullest and the Liberal Alliance seemed the indispensable and only key to Ireland's future, Parnell summoned the members of the Irish town councils together and he made a speech in which he said:

> . . . I will say to you, gentlemen, tonight that if our constitutional movement were to fail . . . if it became evident that we could not by parliamentary action and continued representation at Westminster restore to Ireland the high privilege of self-government . . . I for one would not continue to remain for 24 hours longer in the House of Commons at Westminster . . . the most advanced section of Irishmen as well as the least advanced, have always thoroughly understood that the parliamentary policy was to be a trial and that we did not ourselves believe in the possibility of maintaining for all time, or for any lengthened period, an incorrupt and independent Irish representation at Westminster.

The speech seems so inopportune to Dr Lyons that he casts around — as Dr Conor Cruise O'Brien did before him — for a political motivation for the making of it. After rejecting Dr O'Brien's old gloss as "excessively Machiavellian", even for Parnell, he hazards another explanation of his own and it is only after this has been advanced that he commits himself to the rather astonishing sentence: "The second explanation is that he said what he did because he believed it."

Of course, the rather plain fact of the matter is that while he naturally muted his thoughts on this and other dangerous subjects for quite long periods, as Dr Lyons then more or less proceeds to admit, Parnell throughout his career spoke of the Parliamentary policy as being merely one of a number of options and of the inevitably corrupting effect of indefinitely continued attendance at Westminster in season and out of season. Indeed so far from being primarily devious, or cunning, or over-given to tergiversation or subterfuge, as it is now the fashion to believe, the most striking thing about Parnell is his consistency.

When his career is viewed as a whole and is not broken up into three parts — the early hothead, the mature statesman, the later lunatic — that consistency becomes plain. But the compartmentalisation of Parnell's career is an old game and was played in his time too. Gladstone sought to convince his party in the late eighties that they were dealing with a wise and moderate man who had now repented of the errors of his youth; while after the split it became an obvious ploy to excuse yourself from your former allegiance by declaring that in any case Parnell was no longer the same man and no longer responsible for his words or actions. The truth is, though, that there was only one Parnell; that, like it or lump it, he was a much more extreme and dangerous fellow than the majority of his followers, even those who, like Dillon, had sometimes the name of being a radical where he was moderate; and that the last great period of hopeless defiance is much better seen as a reversion after a long period of enforced concealment of view than it is as a total and inexplicable aberration.

The difference between Parnell and all other parliamentarians before and since is in fact a simple one, as is the difference between Parnell and all other non-republican or non-separatists. Alone among Parliamentarians, he never fell in love with Parliament; and alone among those who did not believe that the connection with England could or should be broken overnight, he never fell in love with the connection. Once this is grasped, there is a great deal that is explained and a great deal that no longer needs explanation, including the air of general bewilderment common among his biographers.

Take, for example, the "hostility" or better still, the "implacable hostility" to England with which they all start and for which most of them advance his mother's influence as explanation. (Dr Lyons avoids this: he sees Magdalen and not being "English in England" as sufficient. In this of course he is reminiscent of Dr O'Brien and others on Yeats's "anti-Englishness".) What puzzles people really is that a reasonable man, who takes the "civilised" view, should believe in the total separation of these two islands. When he is besides a landlord — albeit a fairly uncultured one — the puzzlement is extreme. But a belief in the eventually total separation of these two islands may be a fruit of reason rather than the sort of emotion supposed to be characteristic of the backwoodsman and the bogtrotter.

So far from implying an implacable hostility to England it is not at all inconsistent with affection for the place, for the Irish connection has done England immense harm practically and even more in the world's eyes — a thing which English liberals have been a great deal readier to grasp than Irish ones. The fact that Parnell was almost the only member of the landlord class to make the sort of commitment to Ireland that he made, is proof among other things of his astonishing perspicacity. The ruin of his class and its disappearance as a contributing group to any nation's history has come about simply because it failed to make that commitment.

As a remark to his brother John quoted by Dr Lyons makes clear, Parnell realised that whatever advantages they gained or did not gain from the connection, the attitude of the English governing class to the Irish was basically racist. The Irish were despised by their masters because they had failed to stand up to them; the slave is ever and always despised for his enslavement.

Thus "Parnellism", which might be defined as follows: Ask for what you want as of right and not as dependent to master or client to patron. While always hoping for the best, remember that the relationship is ultimately based on force, and that your opponents are not oblivious of this. To mention force as a factor in the relationship is therefore merely to see it as it is; and to invoke it as a possibility is to do no more than they do all the time. Nevertheless, for the weaker party to appeal to force may simply be to play into the hands of the stronger, though the special relationship of both Britain and Ireland to the United States is a sort of evening-out of the balance.

That this sort of attitude to England and English urbanities can be described as Parnellite does not mean that he invented the tactic of pursuing peace while pointing to the possibility of war. Still less, alas, does it mean that he was ultimately successful in its use. Invent it or not, though, he was astonishingly clear-headed about it from start to finish; and it is this clear-headedness, often mistaken for cynicism, which has had the effect of alienating his more liberal and fuzzy-headed biographers while, paradoxically, making it easier for them to accuse him of playing mere politics for a large part of his career. The companion to the "Machiavellian" Parnell is the "rash" Parnell, or even the daft Parnell; and it is these two figures who inhabit Dr Lyon's book. It is true that they are both balanced to some extent by a third figure, the "statesmanlike" Parnell, but it is noteworthy that he is at his most statesmanlike when he is most moderate and never when he is playing for high stakes.

Of course it is also true to say that Parnell, in a sense quite independent of the divorce action and its outcome, dug his own political grave. The Liberal alliance was a betrayal of the ultimate principles of Parnellism and was the final error in a series which included the Land War and the encouragement of the Irish clergy to believe that they controlled the Irish Party. Out of eventually total dependence on the Liberals, as out of an equal dependence on the bishops and the parish priests, only one result could and did come. Whether the elephantine manner in which Gladstone and Morley handled the crisis when it broke was in truth a product of ineptitude or a reflection of the fact that they had been merely and sedulously playing their own political game all along, makes no difference. In that two pronged dependence, and that reduction of everything to the internal needs and hypocrisies of an English party, lay the seed of failure. Parnell had always known this. He had to some extent avoided the knowledge; and in his "statesmanlike" period he had indeed played politics. That, as the Parnellites always claimed, Gladstone moved first and moved disastrously, whether through cunning or stupidity, is surely beyond dispute. How could Parnell regard the move as other than a confirmation of what he had always believed? And why should he not tell the people so?

Whatever about his political attitudes, the figure that emerges from Dr Lyons's pages is recognisably the one we now know pretty well. The aloof charmer, the mad scientist, the oracular Sherlock Holmes dealing affectionately with some rather obtuse Watsons, the domesticated lover; all are here. The only familiar personification of the legend missing in fact is the one by which Yeats and Joyce set such store.

Though Yeats was undoubtedly correct in seeing him as the alter ego to which slavish, whining, hoping-to-please Ireland gave itself as to an apparent opposite, the saturnine mob-despiser and hater of demos is as absent from Dr Lyons's as from all other pages. Indeed he became, as Dr Lyons demonstates, more, and not less, matey to his inferiors, social and mental, as things went against him. While the middle class, as personified by Healy, remains what it was, the brooding aristocrat who was supposed to be the mob's opponent is missing — as how could he not be since the mob was for him? "I may say that the whole city of Kilkenny turned out last night to receive Parnell," wrote Dr Abraham Brownrigg, the Bishop of Ossory. "The *ladies* (so called) were the most demonstrative of all. The lowest dregs of the people, the

Fenian element and the working classes, are all to a man with Parnell."

Nobody need regret that that particular figment of the literary imagination — fittingly enough, a product of the nineties — is gone. In any case, the lonely mob-hater had been brought about to the end of the literary road and what literary mileage remains to be extracted from Parnell may well be on the personal and domestic side. If Ireland were secure enough in itself — if the connection were finally broken and all the old inferiority gone — a Strachey-like biographer might well have some fun: with the assaying, with the domesticity, with the thought of that inheritance. And what, incidentally, was he up to before he met her, at the ripe old age of thirty-four? Only one symbolic aspect of the Chief ought perhaps to remain sacred. There is in the Irish heart a deep desire for the connection with England to be broken, but to be broken without unnecessary savagery or bloodshed. To those who look like bringing that one off, the Irish people give their hearts. They were mistaken in Parnell, for he failed and was indeed booked for failure from a very long way out. But he had a good enough try all the same.

Dev Contra Mundum

IN THE midst of all the meaningless clichés and soggy tributes on the evening of this day last week came Mr John A. Costello, who said: " . . . his influence was widespread in his life. I think his influence is now at an end." And: "In my opinion he has left nothing of permanent value behind him." On Tuesday my colleague Mr James Downey devoted his column on another page to a lucid summation of what precisely Dev had contributed to the sphere of practical politics and the development of the party system in our democracy. It was an intelligent and, if one confined one's considerations to that sphere, persuasive analysis; but in my opinion Mr Costello was right. Indeed I go further than he did. Not only did Dev leave little or nothing behind him, but in any fundamental sense his influence on his own time as it had to be lived through was extraordinarily limited. His life is in many aspects an object lesson.

In saying this I am remembering of course that it was Dev's party which took the first steps towards the welfare state in the bitter 1930s; that Fianna Fáil's housing schemes of those years are still a notable and — compared to much that came after — a not too reprehensible feature of our urban landscape; and that on a perhaps admittedly more transient level he stopped the annuities, got back the ports, "kept us out of the war," split (or did not split) Sinn Féin twice over, cause (or did not cause) the civil war; and saddled us with a constitution whose irrelevant theological assumptions are as dead as the decrees of the Council of Trent but unfortunately have more binding force in law.

And I am remembering too, in case anybody should think the contrary, that in the even bitterer 1940s and early 1950s many of us fixed on Dev as the Olympian originating source of all the pietism, the nationalist hypocrisy, the craw-thumping, the mixture of complacency and neurosis by which it seemed to us we were ruled; which encouraged the worst and least interesting sides of the Irish character to suck up the proper nourishment of the more freedom-loving and the more fruitful; which made Ireland a narrow and in many respects, a hateful place, and which, it is not too much to say, made each day's newspapers an insult to the sensibility, the sense of honesty and the intelligence.

In this of course we were wrong, for, to be practical about the matter; it was not Dev who had introduced censorship, either legal or gratuitous, inaugurated the disastrous language policy (though of course he continued it), begun the strait-jacketing about the past and what not. Nor, of course, was it Dev who had created the modern puritanism and misogyny of the Irish character in the first place.

But our wrongness in this instance is a case in point, for by whatever alchemy is known to great men Dev had made himself into a symbol of his country; and in so far as all the things listed above were our country we hated him as well as it. By wrapping himself in that long cloak with the silver clasp which made him of the same kindred as Cathleen Ní Houlihan herself, or later in the astounding black overcoat which suggested a final identity of lay and cleric, he had brought that hatred of everything that was allegedly more Irish and more worthy of reverence than any other thing upon himself.

But the hypocrisies and puritanisms just mentioned were not, as has been said, his creation, any more than the attenuated vulgarities which succeeded them were his creation; and no more, probably, than the housing programme, the social policy, the scrapping of the annuities etc. were very much his creation. In the first place, the part of republicanism that Dev took with him into the Dáil had something of the radicalism of all republican tradition about it, and in the second, under our system the scramble for the vacant ground among the voters will ensure that the social policy of the moment will come into existence anyway, give or take confusions and the relative efficiency and drive of the people who undertake to implement it, but otherwise left following right and right following left within narrowly defined limits as the night follows the day.

What is certainly more surprising to reflect on though, and more dismaying to those who believe in the efficacy of the political will, is that in a deep and fundamental sense the Ireland of the time Dev saw to its end came into existence actually contrary in many of its most important aspects to his expressed wishes. Although he was the dominant figure in political Ireland for as long as any of us can remember, the real changes and real developments that came about were not of his initiation: indeed he can be seen to have struggled in a rather forlorn and perhaps rather lonely way against them. The Ireland of this present moment is not the product of his vision, such as it was. The commonwealth in which we dwell may have grown up under his auspices and under his austere eyes, but is not of his making. What he got, and what we all got, was not what he wanted.

What in fact did he want? Well, everybody knows now the famous St Patrick's Day speech about the old men in the chimney corners and the contests of manly youths: indeed many people have presumed to have a good laugh at it. The description of the land of content in it I have summarised elsewhere as a description of an Ireland which should be rural, abstemious, unambitious, uncomplicated and therefore quite unlike the rest of the world; but in so describing it I was wrong, just as anybody who has laughed was wrong; for Dev's hopes for Ireland were not only astounding in their own simple nobility; but they included a hope that Ireland would be in some respects anyway astoundingly ambitious.

Here is what he said in the speech in which he inaugurated the Athlone radio station in February 6th in the fateful year of 1933, when it must have still seemed to him that all was possible and a great deal might come to pass:

> I have spoken at some length of Ireland's history and her contributions to European culture, because I wish to emphasise that what Ireland has done in the past she can do in the future. The Irish genius has always stressed spiritual and intellectual rather than material values. That is the characteristic that fits the Irish people in a special manner for the task, now a vital one, of helping to save Western civilisation. The great material progress of recent times, coming in a world where false philosophies already reigned, has distorted men's sense of proportion; the material has usurped the sovereignty that is the right of the spiritual. Everywhere today the consequences of this perversion of the natural order are to be seen. Spirit and mind have ceased to rule. The riches which the world sought, and to which it sacrificed all else, have become a curse by their very abundance.
>
> In this day, if Ireland is faithful to her mission and, please God she will be, if as of old she recalls men to forgotten truths, if she places before them the ideals of justice, of order, of freedom rightly used, of Christian brotherhood — then, indeed, she can do the world a service as great as that which she rendered in the time of Columcille and Columbanus, because the need of our time is in no ways less.
>
> You sometimes hear Ireland charged with a narrow and intolerant Nationalism, but Ireland today has no dearer hope than this: that, true to her own holiest traditions, she may humbly serve the truth and help by truth to save the world.

It is possible to see this as merely another assertion of the divinely ordained mission of Irish Catholicism, though in fact it comes at the end of an address in which Dean Swift, Edmund Burke, Oliver Goldsmith and *(mirabile dictu)* Wiliam Carleton are mentioned, along with the Gaelic poets of the 18th century. It is certain that many will find it risible. To regard it in either light would, however, be wrong, for Dev had it in his heart that Ireland would go a much stranger path than that which it has gone: and would hold by an entirely different set of values. Such an Ireland would be frugal, it is true; abstemious and even puritanical; and it would have the rural small-holding supplemented by native and natively owned industry as the basis of its economy; but to say that it would not have ambition as its motivating force would also be to misdescribe it, for its cultural and intellectual no less than its spiritual ambitions would be boundless and in its combination of such values it might save the world by its example. How far we were from that vision when he died last week in his 93rd year and in which direction we have all the time been travelling, all those who care may judge for themselves.

And that he was true to the simplicity and strength of his vision I have not much doubt, for it is the one consistency that appears and re-appears almost to the end. It is also clear that he had little or no idea of the forces at large in the world (and, if you like, in the hearts of men) which would prevent him or prevent anybody from bringing that dream about; and no conception whatever of a political machinery that would accomplish what would amount to nothing less than a miracle. And though the truth is that nothing could even have retarded for long the forces which would have destroyed in any case his conception, it may yet be salutory to set out the heads of what may have been his confusions.

It is probable that he saw an essentially frugal and religious minded peasant proprietorship as an ideal basis for what he had in mind when the fact is that peasant proprietorship is a breeding ground for acquisitiveness, discontent, apathy and acceptance of economic failure in varying proportions; that its spiritual values consist merely in a craven regard for priesthood; and that it is in any case a pathetic and useless barrier against modern economic forces. It is probable that he saw, without much reference to the economic basis of the thing, urban Irishness as being in some way spiritualisable because of Ireland's history and traditions of sacrifice and resolve. We know that under private enterprise and corporate capitalism at the present stage of the world's development urban man is essentially an individual in whom "civic man", "economic man" and *l'homme moyen sensuel* co-exist in uneasy partnership, the whole making some sort of occasional obeisance to his tribal deities, or confusing his religious feelings with the "social conscience" that belongs to the civic side of him.

In all the statements that have the ring of the ultimate Dev about them we can see quite clearly that in so far as he has any conception of the difference, he sets a higher value upon the nation than upon the state. Yet given modern conditions it was nothing less than inevitable that he should have presided over the growth of the state with its preposterous machinery while the idea of the nation fled elsewhere for sustenance.

The list is long. It could of course be longer. We could speak of education, the language *in vacuo,* the economics of art, intellectual endeavour and much else. More to the point perhaps we could also speak of these confusions in other terms: discuss, as James Downey and John A. Costello did, Dev's notion of the processes of British parliamentary democracy as being somehow God-given and go on to discuss whether the sort of vision which he had falls within the proper sphere of such politics at all. We could speak too of protectionism versus internationalism and free trade; and of the related question of whether such corruptions as he feared, foreign cultural domination and the appeal of certain forms of commercialised entertainment and communication can be brought under any sort of control while the profit motive exists to further them. We could in these contexts discuss the differences between Sean Lemass's eventual Ireland and Dev's dream, pointing to the fact that Lemass's Ireland was simply what the island of destiny was bound to become when the economics which prevail elsewhere were welcomed openly and frankly through its portals. But to do all this might be, in a way, to add our own confusions to Dev's. His, perhaps, went deeper; and they were, I suggest, essentially tragic ones.

The Failure of Jim Larkin

JIM LARKIN is not among the figures included in Dr Conor Cruise O'Brien's compendium, *The Shaping of Modern Ireland,* in which Connolly and Pearse are (rather inadequately) dealt with together by Dorothy McArdle, but there may be a sense in which the Doctor was right to leave him out. In one important way, whatever adulation is accorded to his memory, and however the years between are summed up by the various functionaries and pundits who will take notice of the centenary now at hand, Big Jim is not among the makers of modern Ireland. And if his ghost stalks – as in one sense or another it will always continue to stalk – the streets of Dublin, it must be at least as much a disconsolate and forlorn as a triumphant or a happy spirit.

In saying this of course one can hardly be other than aware that a building called "Liberty Hall" dominates the skyline; that trade union membership is in the region of 400,000; that the standard of living of manual workers (and of a great many other people too) bears no relationship to that of 1907 or 1913; that the old tenement slums, which in the year of his death still encroached on Stephen's Green, have been abolished; and that the power of organised unionism is felt in every branch of industry.

Of all these things we shall doubtless be often enough reminded, and the reminders will not emanate only from his heirs and opposite numbers (if that is what they be) in Liberty Hall, nor only from those in the more direct line of succession in 29 Parnell Square. The climate of contemporary Ireland is, in spite of the events of the last few years, still a smug and socially complacent one; and the comparisons which will be drawn during his centenary between conditions then and now will not be drawn only by the big-wigs of the Labour Party or by others who feel they have a vested interest in the matter.

Achievement-measuring is a game that all too many of us are good at; and the measurers will come from all shades of the political spectrum. They will include clerics as well as laymen and those who might be roughly described as being conservatives as well as those who might be still more roughly described as being of the left. Statistics will be produced again about infant mortality, the number of families living in one room in 1913 and other matters, including even real wages, which will show the distance we have travelled in terms of what will doubtless be called social justice as well as social compassion. And for the most part these comparisons will be well drawn. There are things to be proud of, though who is to be proud of them except the organised workers themselves, is another matter. And yet, withal, in this year of his centenary, Jim Larkin remains a failure.

There is no question of course but that he would be pleased with the changes in material conditions such as they are, and whatever their degree of absoluteness or relativity. That he had himself a firm grasp of the economic side of unionism is indubitable: indeed it was in this firm grasp of the difference between betterment and the status quo ante that much of his great greatness lies. And as far as the other things are concerned, nothing that his enemies said of him was truer than that when he sought a wider application of his vision he almost invariably turned out to be both disruptive and destructive. Not only was it true that he was rather an inept politician; but it was also very obviously the case that, like many a socialist before and since, he had no clear grasp of how, or by what means, a transition to socialism was to be managed. R.M. Fox said he "belonged to the English school of Socialism" in the sense that he "always had a disregard for social theory"; and, indeed, though almost every utterance that Big Jim ever made proves that he understood quite clearly and passionately what socialism was, almost every other utterance proves that he had likewise only very hazy ideas as to how it might come about.

There were indubitably elements of Syndicalism, with or without the capital S in his thinking; as — however unfashionable it may be to say — there also were in Connolly's; although in Connolly's thinking they were, like everything else perhaps, much more clearly defined. Without becoming too sectarian about it Syndicalism might be stated as the belief that the trade union (ideally the "one big union") should not only be the centre of the class struggle, but also the nucleus of the new society.

Connolly put the essence of the matter graphically enough when he said:

> Let us be clear as to the function of Industrial Unionism. That function is to build up an industrial republic inside the shell of the political state, in order that when the industrial republic is fully organised it may crack the shell of the political state and step into its place in the scheme of the universe.

But whether or not syndicalists believed that trade unions ("industrial unions" as they would have said) in their very organisational essence were to be paradigms of the new society to come;

all were agreed that unionism had a political dimension as well as an economic one and that, without sacrificing the immediate interests of the workers, the purpose of trade union organisation and action was to bring about the end of capitalist society.

The dream weapon of pure Snydicalism on the French and Spanish model was therefore the General Strike. When the moment was ripe the General Strike would bring about a sudden and bloodless transition to Socialism; and according to my colleague Claud Cockburn in a fascinating study of some aspects of 20th century unionism in England published some months ago, *Union Power: The Growth and Challenge in Perspective,* it was an understanding among the left militants who actually led the strikes between 1907 and the outbreak of the war in 1914, sometimes in opposition to the official leadership, that these were to culminate in a revolutionary General Strike scheduled for September 1914. Cockburn goes on to suggest that the knowledge of this in establishment circles may have caused them to look with favour on a conflict with Germany; but more to our present purpose he says with apparent plausibility that the betrayal of Larkin and the Dublin workers by the British TUC resulted from the fact that "some of the British trade union leaders were terrified by Larkin's open Syndicalism, and others sceptical of the entire Syndicalist concept."

Whether or not Larkin's Syndicalist ideas were ever very clearly thought out, and Fox probably has the right of it in saying that he was (in a way that is, after all, more characteristic of "English" Socialism than of "Continental") at all stages short on theory, they were seemingly abandoned after the Russian revolution had brought a socialist regime into existence by other means: though how those other means were to be translated or applied in the apparent democracies remained as unclear to him as it did even to large numbers of others who viewed events in Russia with favour and joined Communist parties elsewhere in Europe. Nor is Syndicalism what it was, its connection with the ideas of Georges Sorel, no less than with those of Mussulini, the corporatists and certain varieties of anarchists having effectively discredited it in the eyes of large segments of the international left, while Ernest Bevin and his colleagues ruthlessly crushed what remained of it in British trade unionism and the British Labour Party in the 1920s and '30s.

But whether or not Jim Larkin was ever in any real, doctrinaire sense a Syndicalist, the truth is that other than Syndicalists believed in 1913, and certainly Jim Larkin believed with every particle of his being, that trade unionism — or industrial unionism — had a more important function than betterment within the system. Organised workers were to him "pioneers of a newer time"; and unless every struggle was also an educative struggle; unless it increased the workers' grasp and sense of their own power to bring about a fundamental change; unless it magnified their revolutionary class consciousness and depth and degree of class solidarity; it was, in the ultimate sense, a failure. And who shall say that the effectual class consciousness of organised unionism today is greater than he miraculously brought about in the years leading up to 1913? Trade union leadership is on the whole, in a way that would have shocked Larkin, content with things as they are; nor does it ever seriously envisage the weapons in its armoury as weapons to bring about a complete transformation of society along socialist lines. No less than does its equivalent in Britain, established Irish trade union leadership would, by all the signs, retreat from the brink if the brink ever appeared in view; and in the sense that the organisations that sprang from his living word do not share his living vision, Jim Larkin is a failure.

But the failure, whether it is primarily a matter of union leadership or not, goes deeper. Larkin himself did not want a trade union leadership which would drag its organised members into a struggle for change which would only distract from its immediate betterment or lead to the collapse of its immediate hopes. He was never guilty of playing with the working class in the sense which the common contemporary description of him as an agitator would suggest, or the way in which certain middle-class socialists who look upon it unrealistically as a weapon of their individual dreams would like to do. But every time he brought workers out for better wages he was at pains to emphasise that their action was bringing an end of the wages system itself a day or two nearer. Every time he spoke of class betterment he spoke also of liberation from the chains of class itself. The strike may have been a primary weapon; but the primary object remained an awakening which would go beyond the immediate causes of the strike or the immediate conditions of its settlement. That awakening, for whatever reason, has not come about, and though ultimately conservative theorists may continue to suggest that revolutionary aspirations will always vanish when the Hondas and the coloured television sets come within people's grasp, to say that that happens in any country where it does happen (and it must be emphasised over and over again that it does not happen universally or even in countries near at hand) may be simply to put the blame more squarely where it lies: with the leadership of the working class, whether trade union or parliamentary.

That leadership has certainly on balance failed Larkin and failed in what used to be called Larkinism. The causes of the failure may be many and, as far as the leadership is concerned, they may reside in part at least in the tangled history of the splits which Big Jim had his part in creating. But it exists nonetheless, and the consciousness of it should be present — no less than his ghost itself — in this city at this time. Big Jim was a socialist; and while it may be true that reasons other than a growth in the revolutionary consciousness of the working class may help to bring socialism about; it cannot come about without it or in spite of its absence. The extent of its absence may or may not be the measure of the degree to which, even with their access to the media, their educative activities and everything else, his successors have failed him; but to that extent anyway, he has had little or no influence on the making of modern Ireland.

Farewell Kiltartan

YEATS, AS we all know, thought highly of the peasantry and not much of the middle classes. I say "as we all know" although in a solemn disputation in *The Crane Bag* between the two rival candidates for the Professorship of Anglo-Irish Literature (whatever that may be) in UCD, one of them, Dr Deane, announces the fact so portentously that you might think he had discovered it, or at the very least that it had been discovered only yesterday. Still, never mind.

The truth is the rest of us knew it more or less in our cradles; and knew too, even if only in a vague sort of way suited to our non-professorial ambitions and station in life, what lay behind it: "New from the influence, mainly the personal influence, of William Morris, I dreamed of enlarging Irish hate, till we had come to hate with a passion of patriotism what Morris and Ruskin hated."

The statement is not without nobility; and we could certainly do nowadays with a little more hate all round, as well as a good deal less cant; but the key phrase is "what Morris and Ruskin hated." Morris and Ruskin were, in Yeats's youth, the chief latter day ideologists of that hatred of the industrial and mercantile revolution which had been common ground for poets and literary men of all descriptions from William Blake down to Yeats's "companions of the Chesire Cheese". The hatred was not only for the forms and evidences of what the bourgeoisie looked upon as material progress, "the dark Satanic mills", the machine-made furniture and the rest of it, but for the mentality that went with them. It was to go on being more or less common ground into the days of the Chester-Belloc and even D.H. Lawrence, although some time after the era of Ruskin and Morris and Carlyle the influence of Marx began to penetrate even to some who had not read him so that it began to dawn even on poets and literary men that the industrial and mercantile revolution might have been a sort of real progress after all.

Still, in the late Victorian era which was the time of Yeats's youth, that hatred was at a high pitch. There was something about the level of material comfort and prosperity which certain classes had attained in the late Victorian era, and the self-satisfied assumptions that it bred, which moved literary men to a special sort of rage.

Mostly this rage had a Messianic dimension: Carlyle and Ruskin and Morris believed that by preaching and propaganda, a revolution could be brought about. It would be a backward-looking revolution, enshrining the values of that fictionalised and idealised Middle Ages which everybody since Walter Scott had believed in, but it would be a revolution all the same. By preaching, the belief went, at the wives and daughters of the money-changers, and at such "working men" as would listen, the money-changers would be driven from the temple; and if you were an active, socially-minded man, with a bias towards active politics and propaganda, such as William Morris was, that belief saved you from despair, or at least from the feeling that you were merely "an idle singer of an idle day".

But there were others who were not so actively minded; and they too were among Yeats's friends. Heirs to a tradition of withdrawal from the busy, ugly, ruthless and insensitive contemporary world which in "The Tragic Generation" he traces back to Keats and Coleridge, but in which he might, if he had been at that point inclined, have included Baudelaire, their only refuges were religion and drink.

> What portion in the world can the artist have,
> Who has awaked from the common dream
> But dissipation and despair?

And in the 'eighties and 'nineties, Yeats, as far as what Patrick Kavanagh used to call "the London end of things" was concerned, had, to some extent at least, a foot in both camps. As late as 1922 he was to say, looking back, that Morris, at whose house incidentally he attended the debates of the Socialist League and met Bernard Shaw, had "a spontaneity and joy" that "made him my chief of men." "Today I do not set his poetry very high, but for an odd altogether wonderful line or thought; and yet, if some angel offered me the choice, I would choose to live his life, poetry and all, rather than my own or any other man's."

But nevertheless he had, as has been said, friends who were not so active, unless debauchery and dissipation may be counted activities, and they were among his chief of men too. Lionel Johnson and Ernest Dowson, who like a host of others, "faced their ends when young," were the ones who had most symbolic significance for him in later years. This admiration for an active man like Morris, whose "dream world was as much the antithesis of daily life as with other men of genius," but who "was never conscious of the antithesis and so knew nothing of intellectual suffering" and the profound respect he showed always for those who were faithful to their sufferings as to nothing else, Cynaras and first loves included, beautifully reflected a dichotomy in Yeats's own nature. For he was himself pre-eminently a dreamer and would-be man of action at the same time. Much of his life is a record of his attempt to escape from the toils of dream; most of his thought centres round contradictions in his own nature; and of all his dichotomies and contradictions this one was the most persistent.

Now it would not be fair to say that for someone conscious of this contradiction, who admired Ruskin's "Unto This Last" and was attracted to theosophy at the same time, Ireland, at a certain stage, offered a way out. There was, after all, the acquaintance with John O'Leary; there were Standish O'Grady and Samuel Ferguson; there were "The Wanderings of Oisín"; there was the advent of "a lady of great height as radiant as Flora herself," named Maud Gonne in a hansom cab at 8 Blenheim Road, and there was, above all, whatever notions we may have about the existence of such a thing as Anglo-Irish literature, the fact of Irishness itself. But nevertheless for someone who regarded the contemporary world with profound dismay (as everyone else did) but who was inclined to suspect (as some of his friends did) that the Ruskin-Morris thing, the medieval socialist thing and the activist thing was an illusion, Ireland did in a sense offer a way out, for in Ireland the past was still alive. You did not have to recreate it by preaching to the hated middle classes, by vulgar newspaper propaganda and pamphleteering, by soap-box oratory of one kind or another. And, as part of the living past which was to be found in Ireland, there was the peasantry — or, as Yeats more often said, the country-people or the common people:

> Mitchel had already poured some of that hate drawn from Carlyle ... into the blood of Ireland, and were we not a poor nation with ancient courage, unblackened fields and a barbarous gift of self-sacrifice? Ruskin and Morris had spent themselves in vain because they found no passion to harness to their thought, but here were unwasted passions and precedents in the popular memory for every needed thought and action. Perhaps too it would be possible to find in that new philosophy of spiritism coming to a seeming climax in the work of Frederick Myers, and in the investigations of uncounted obscure persons, what could change the country spiritism into a reasoned belief that would put its might into all the rest. A new belief seemed coming that could be so simple and demonstrable, and above all so mixed into the common scenery of the world, that it would set the whole man on fire and liberate him from a thousand obediences and complexities. We were to forge in Ireland a new sword on our old traditional anvil for that great battle that must in the end re-establish the old, confident joyous world.

Ah, that liberation from "obediences and complexities"! How it betrays us and how it recedes as we seem almost to have found it! Yeats was an extremely intelligent and, in his own particular way, a dazzlingly honest man. He soon had his doubts and as early as 1907 he was expressing them. There was, it seemed a new class in Ireland, and a new type of mind, "which had been without influence in the generation of Grattan, and almost without it in that of Davis" and it was taking over. This was the dreaded middle-class again, though still at the clerk and shopkeeper stage. It had risen above the traditions of the countryman without learning those of cultivated life, or even educating itself.

Because of its poverty, its ignorance and its superstitious piety it was much subject to all kinds of fear; and Yeats's hatred of the cowardice and play-safe mentality of this new class reached a climax in 1913 in what is still, let it be said, a great poem; the one about romantic Ireland being dead and gone.

But if the representatives of the new middle class were afraid of the priest and others because of "their poverty, their ignorance and their superstitious piety," what, it might at this distance of time be asked, about the country people? Were they not poor, ignorant and superstitious too? The answer really was in two parts. One was in the traditional wisdom and lore, the immemorial folk-memories and language of the peasantry. The other, strangely enough was in their even greater poverty. They had, it seemed, literally nothing:

> Aristocrats have made beautiful manners, because their place in the world puts them above the fear of life, and the countrymen have made beautiful stories and beliefs, because they have nothing to lose and so do not fear, and the artists have made all the rest because Providence has filled them with recklessness.

In this, of course, Yeats was quite literally mistaken, and as he went around the cottages with Lady Gregory, he should have found out. The peasantry already had quite a little bit to lose and had had since the early eighties (some of them much longer). If his patron had been the lady of the manor in a more prosperous part than Clare-Galway, it should have been obvious. Perhaps they visited only the poorer houses.

In any case what Yeats — who, whatever his disillusionments, maintained his belief in the peasantry in one way or another to the end — left out of account was that there was not much difference between a peasant property owner and a middle-class shopkeeper. So far from there being a gulf between the landed peasant and the gombeen man, the two are one and the same fellow with one and the same religion.

Yet whatever excuse there was for Yeats, there is none for us now. Even if it is in any sense true that we were, taking us as a whole, "a poor nation with ancient courage, unblackened fields and a barbarous gift of self-sacrifice" we are so no longer. In spite of 1916 and its aftermath (because you might say, of its aftermath) it should be patently obvious to us now that romantic Ireland is finally dead and gone. It is with O'Leary (who would have no truck with the Land League) in the grave. The way forward is, like it or not, through the transmogrification of the middle class itself and through the harnessing of the third industrial revolution to our own purposes, and not in folk-flummery, druidicisms or the local equivalents of morris dancing. There may be enough of something or other left to ensure that:

> We in coming days may be
> Still the indomitable Irishry

but the way forward is the way forward, not the way back. And like all ways forward, it will of course be full of complexities and contradictions.

The Cradle of the Race

IN THE current Royal Hibernian Academy exhibition there is a painting by the late John Keating called "Cradle of a Nation". Except for the overall brown effect which academics once misguidedly gave their work, it is (which would not, admittedly, be difficult) a painting of a good deal more character and merit than most of what is on view: the interior of a small farm-house, with dresser and press and a stairs up to the loft.

At first I thought the title indicated in a rather subtle way that the cottage or small farmhouse of which this was the interior had been the birth-place of one of our national leaders; and in my own mind I allowed that it must be the famous cottage in Bruree, which, sad to say, I have never clapped an eye on.

But, as I was leaving the place, a knowledgeable acquaintance assured me that it was not so. (That was not at the opening, incidentally. I am not on that list.) It was, he said, merely a small farm-house of which the painter had knowledge, a step above the Bruree class of things, but not much; and the painter's point had been that we all had our origin, not too long ago, in such humble abodes.

If this was indeed the reason for the title (and I dare say it was) Mr Keating was reflecting nothing more or less than a myth which was once very powerful in these parts. All our proximate forebears, the myth said, belonged to the small farmer class. They were all hornyhanded sons of toil who lived in the most humble circumstances; and since they did not even, until very recent times, own the holdings from which they extracted their livelihood, they were all men of no property. They endured the same hardship, ate the same food, feared the same landlords. As far as the material things of life were concerned, we all had the same experience behind us and it was a pretty harsh one.

But the myth went further than this. The Irish people, it said (it meant of course the Irish people who were of southern, Catholic stock, but it did not quite say that) had a good deal more to nourish them than the potato. They had a simple piety, a common cultural experience and a solidarity in the face of misfortune without which they could not have survived. They had all gone to the national school; they all said the rosary at their mother's knee; they all had a folk-memory of better things.

Now in thus having a myth which would bind them together the southern Irish of the Free State era and afterwards were not alone among the peoples of the world. Ever since the days of Romulus and Remus nationality has been very much a matter of shared ancestry; and after the arrival of the Celts the ruling classes in Ireland affectedly shared a common descent from the sons of Milesius. The suggestion that everybody is, or has been, in the same boat is common. All Americans, even those who know the facts to be otherwise, have an ante-natal experience at the frontier.

The binding power of the latter-day, post-Milesian myth in Ireland, though, comes not from the suggestion that we all had noble blood in our veins — however desirable it might be to think that too — but from the assertion that since we all came from the same humble stock, and all had the same experience of misery and exploitation, there had not been any class distinctions amongst us; and, more important there would not be in the future. That two-pence ha'penny had a tendency to look down on two-pence most people admitted; but they felt that that could be quickly corrected by reminding two-pence ha'penny of the facts.

And the myth even, in a funny sort of way, suggested that as a national characteristic we lacked the sort of individual ambition to get on which produces classes and rulers. We had something called spiritual values which ruled that sort of thing out. We knew that, on balance, the simple life was the best; and in the long nights after Samhain we were content with simple, and for the most part chaste, pleasures. We did not lust, and we never had lusted after the fleshpots of Egypt or anywhere else. Even the possession of an education, which people everywhere else in the world (except perhaps the Welsh valleys) knew to be a weapon of advancement, was to us merely a matter of racial pride and mutual uplifting. You did not batter your brains out over the books, or make the requisite sacrifices so that your offspring might do so, merely because there were jobs attached to the results. You did it cum glóire Dé agus onóra na hÉireann, and so that Éireann might be a shining light to the world in respect of the learning as in almost every other respect imaginable.

Well, we know now that it wasn't so: and although some of us suspected it long ago from reading William Carleton and others, it has only fairly recently come as a blinding shock to the historians. There were indeed vital distinctions of class and interest among the rural populations of Ireland in the bad old days; distinctions between the landless labourers who had nothing at all, the small-holders who barely hung on to miserable plots, the larger farmers who had leases and the others who were merely tenants at will.

And these differences were not only between individuals in the same locality, but between area and area. The bare, inhospitable and overcrowded places of the Atlantic seaboard, from which every year the spailpíns set out to look for employment elsewhere, had a different racial and historical experience from that of many people who lived among richer pastures.

And not only were there different levels of experience among different classes in the rural community but there were bitter and sometimes bloody conflicts of interest among them too. In the bad old days in Ireland, not only did two-pence ha'penny look down on two-pence, but he squeezed him and exploited him and dispossessed him of his few miserable acres whenever he could. And two-pence (or no pence at all) struck back, often in blind ferocity and hate.

And, as some of us could have told the historians also from reading Griffin and the Banim brothers and others, there was, from the late 18th century on, a Catholic middle-class growing up in the towns which had very definite and snobbish ideas about social status and advantage and which regarded the sort of education for which it was prepared to fork-out money to the eager clergy as the key to further escalation of the ladder. After the passage of the Encumbered Estates Act in 1849 some of them even went back to the land as graziers and landlords; and pretty hard-fisted gentlemen they proved.

The importance and the relevance (in case you are wondering) of all this is (you will be glad to hear) quite simple: it is a mistake to think of the Irish people as somehow not addicted to class distinctions; and it is equally a libel on them to think of them as necessarily besotted by ideas of the simple life. Class distinctions there were, among the Catholic majority itself; and individual ambition and advantage-seeking a-plenty; while the only reason there was an apparent affection for the simple life was that the simple life was the only one available. If the fleshpots had been anywhere within reach they would have lusted after them; and as a glance around will show when the conditions are favourable and the ethos begins to encourage it the Irish are as self-seeking as anybody else; and as vulgar and as materialistic and as clownish in their pursuits.

Still, the myth was there and had a power of its own. It contributed to history as well as being a reading of it; and it is now reckoned in some quarters to be dangerous. Because it was, as much as anything else, a myth of shared suffering, and therefore is adjudged to be possible fuel for nationalist and revengeful flames, some historians are at the moment rather overdoing the de-bunking of the cradle of the race idea. Accordingly, when one reads discussions on the matter, one should always look for the figures and read the small print. There was no county in Ireland on the eve of the famine in which there was not a preponderance of "farms" of under fifteen acres; and in many of them the size of the majority of holdings was under five. The Catholic middle class was infinitesiminal by the standards of the "middle class" of today; and it began to emerge rather later than some of our newly awakened historians are now suggesting. For the ancestors of the vast majority of us (including, up to a certain point, the Presbyterians of Ulster) degradation, exploitation and servitude were facts of life; and the particular sort of degradation and exploitation that was suffered by the majority of the Irish people was, like it or not, a more or less direct product of the British connection.

One final point though. It has been, for the most part, the descendants of the landless or the nearly landless who have been forced out. What has been happening in fairly recent times has been in many ways equivalent to a gigantic process of clearance in favour of the more privileged. The present middle class is probably amost entirely descended from the less desperate and less destitute, those who were somewhat more comfortably off than others and those who began the process of education early. If emigration is — as, one can only assume, the authors of the recent Green Paper think it will be, resumed — they may well, in time, come to have the country to themselves and in that case the myth of a common sort of ancestry will, up to a point, come true.

What You Voted For

THE STRUCTURE of Irish politics is dictated by the civil war; its over-all tendencies and its innate conservatism by the Land Acts, the greatest disaster of recent Irish history. Before the civil war there was Sinn Féin, the name under which the more eager nationalist elements, including those who had taken part in 1916 and those who decided to approve of it merely in retrospect and for policy purposes, had agreed to come together after the rising. The name Sinn Féin had belonged to Arthur Griffith, whose attitude to 1916 had been ambiguous, to say the least, but who had been lucky enough to be arrested by the British, and he now yielded it up with mixed feelings to the I.R.B. men, to those republicans, who, like Cathal Brugha, were not members of the I.R.B. family, and to the Catholic Gaelic nationalists of whom for so long de Valera was to be the representative figure.

There were already deep divisions within the ranks of this re-born Sinn Féin; and much has of late been made of them, as by F.S.L. Lyons in *Ireland Since The Famine*; but in a way they are misleading divisions. With the death of Connolly the organised proletarian left had ceased to participate in advanced nationalist politics; organised, sworn Fenianism as represented by the I.R.B. had long been conservative in everything but its attitude to physical force and "the republic" which it was eventually to betray; and the agrarian left which was represented in the ranks of the new movement had only rudimentary ideas. Although the first Dáil gave lip-service to an advanced social programme which incorporated radical phrases from Pearse's writings, that was soon forgotten. Indeed, compared to most of the leadership of the new Sinn Féin Pearse was a social extremist whose ideas were better forgotten, while Connolly was nothing more or less than a red.

In fact, instead of concentrating on the divisions in the renascent nationalist movement it is better to see it as one thing — one peasant proprietorial and middle-class thing, with overtones of industrial nationalism as heretofore preached by Arthur Griffith and subsequently by Seán Lemass: and it would certainly not be going too far to say either that the divisions between it and the old nationalist party have been misleadingly exaggerated. A figure like Kevin O'Higgins, with his Healy-Sullivan connections, his unremitting legalism and his love of the British-model parliamentary process may stand as representative of the fact that whatever their attitude to the hoary old question of physical force versus negotiation, the gap between the Irish Nationalist Party and certain elements in the new Sinn Féin was really little more than a generation gap, with all that that implies in the way of impatience with old methods and perhaps even an infusion of something to be called idealism.

When the Sullivans and Healys were younger they, too, had sung, and even written, their death or glory songs; nor was the emptier rhetoric of the nationalist party different in essence from the empty but dangerous rhetoric of which Dr O'Brien tirelessly accuses Fianna Fáil. Peasant proprietorial and emergent middle-class nationalism is much more of a seamless continuum than we generally think; and it is not entirely an accident that just as the later divisions within Sinn Féin itself looked like having come to the end of their tether as a simultaneously confusing and de-fusing factor in Irish politics, the older division (which was, in essence, only one of the tactics) between the Nationalist Party and its Sinn Féin successors has been resuscitated and made the subject of an unending song and dance.

Sinn Féin, as we all know, won a great victory in 1918, having been solidly unified by the British Government and the fear of conscription. It combined an old appeal to American sentiment — much more effective now that America had proved itself the major power on the world's surface — with an old appeal of arms and quite a considerable recourse to British Liberal opinion: not any longer, it is true, exercised through Parliament, but exercised through the Liberal and Labour Parties and their organs of opinion nonetheless. It won, through these means, a settlement of a sort; and then it split into two wings. From that split, and the resultant two wings created, Fianna Fáil and Fine Gael derive. They are both ultimately the creatures of peasant and middle-class nationalism. They are both the prisoners of the peasant conservatism which became the ruling power in Ireland with the Land Acts.

It is true that the split only came about because Sinn Féin had a radical wing, not led by Mr de Valera, which rejected the "settlement" largely imposed by the British. This radical republican wing had revolutionary elements in it; and it was the representative, in so far as they had a representative, of the still landless elements, which had been excluded from the earlier settlements of the land war; but largely because the Labour movement had been taken out of the nationalist fold after Connolly's death and Larkin's defection to America, it had no urban allies and not much ideology. Before the civil war's end most of the radical leadership had gone to join the dead radicals of 1916; and after 1927, when Fianna Fáil more or less accepted the "treaty" settlement, this radical wing remained in the extra-Parliamentary, republican wilderness.

And yet a radical tradition survived in Fianna Fáil to a sufficient extent to allow the landless men and the hungrier peasantry to identify with it. More important even, and peculiarly enough, it was Fianna Fáil which inherited the industrial nationalism of Griffith's original Sinn Féin, while Fine Gael became the inheritors of the lawyer's nationalism of the Irish parliamentary party, with allies to begin with in conservative Protestant industrial and business circles. This industrial nationalism in Fianna Fáil eventually became its main driving force. It created sufficient wealth and jobs and houses for Fianna Fáil to obtain the allegiance of large sections of the urban proletariat and to maintain its rural-radical image largely by the simple expedient of doles and handouts; but it also decided its fate; for it was through this industrial nationalism that Fianna Fáil became in the modern sense a conservative (i.e. a pro-finance and capital) party with a resultant doom in the sands of speculatordom.

And, of course, as Fianna Fáil became in this sense a conservative party, so Fine Gael became apparently, for a while, a social reformist one, with a large constituency among those of the salaried middle-class who disliked Fianna Fáil's image as a speculator's party and who had social consciences partly because social consciences were fashionable things to have in the 1960s. This made easier the alliance with the Labour Party and gave it a progressivist social tone which was more than Fianna Fáil had the time or the intelligentsia for in the 60s and early 70s. Five years in office have, however, revealed the latent conservatism of Fine Gael, which differs from Fianna Fáil conservatism only in being representative of an older, more "respectable" business tradition, with a slight bias against concession-farming and speculatordom, as well as in tracing back to the first wave of the Catholic middle class to be emancipated, mostly the lawyer class, a fact which also accounts for its greater appearance of culture and sophistication.

As it stands, neither party quite knows where its constituency is supposed to be, nor how it differs from the other lot's. The very small farmer and farm labourer class which used to support Fianna Fáil has been to a large extent driven off the land and out of the country — by the E.E.C. of course, but before that as much by Fianna Fáil's doles and emigration formula as by Fine Gael's general support of the rancher-farmer class. Since it went off to become part of Britain's proletariat its allegiance was never transformed into anything else; and the influx into Dublin has been largely an emancipated peasant turned middle-class influx, partly the result of deliberate middle-class job creation, in the civil service and elsewhere.

Support among those who have remained on the land is, however, vital for both parties; and although the larger the farmer the more he is likely to be a Fine Gael supporter, large and small are all conservatives and impose an iron conservatism on the two major parties when it comes to the "liberal" or reformist issues. Ultimate conservatism probably became a law of life for the satisfied elements in the nationalist mainstream once the land war had been won, and so it dates a long way back, much further back than 1916, which was, in a way, an interruption of a consolidating process.

Those who had fought the good fight, which good fight was inextricably entwined with the ownership of the land, remained nationalist because they were in the process of transforming themselves into a middle class and they wanted the overt control of education, the civil service, the professions and, of course, finance and industry, which independence and its politics would confer on them. When the split came it was largely therefore between two sections of a broadly conservative mass. Of course there were real social issues for a while underlying it and it was largely brought about by the more genuine radicals in the nationalist tradition, as 1916 had been largely brought about.

With that initial radicalism Fianna Fáil remained tinged for many years and it always seems, to those who hope for new alignments, that elements in Fianna Fáil might strike out to recover it. At least it does not appear logical to have two conservative parties, even with the Labour Party restraining one of them. Further splits in the original Sinn Féin mass might well be thought desirable.

The Easy Years

SINCE THE late 1950s at least those who were, broadly speaking, members of the southern Irish middle class have been among the world's fortunate. A moderate amount of business acumen, a professional qualification, a university degree even, have paid dividends which were, judged by the common experience of humanity, wildly disproportionate to the amount of talent or industry actually displayed. For success in whole areas of southern life, in what is called administration, for example, no specific talents of any description were required beyond perhaps the ability to pass an initial entrance examination; while those whose parents had already distinguished themselves through patriotic activities, in the professions, or in business, could look forward to rewarding careers and advancement almost as of right.

The rewards were, in most cases, it is true, not as high as those attainable in the United States or on the continent of Europe. The advantages of inheritance were not quite as great as they are in Saudi Arabia or the Yemen. But of recent years at least almost everybody who came from the urban middle classes or left the farm for them could and did look forward to comforts, decencies and securities which, by the standards of history, and of what they were led to believe was the history of their own forebears in particular, put them among the blessed.

Nor were there advantages lacking over places apparently more fortunate. To rise high in the national life of Ireland, to establish one's niche, to secure the sort of local fame that the not too ambitious are for the most part content to enjoy, to acquire a reputation in one's own field was not as difficult as it might turn out to be in the more metropolitan nations.

Since Ireland is a small country which yet has to have the things which larger countries maintain, there was plenty of room at the top. Since we have, and are entitled to have, on a national scale, such playthings and amusements as radio and television there was, in proportion to population, more chance of becoming, say, a radio or television producer than there was elsewhere. But since the responsibilities (or whatever you like to call them) were the same, the rewards had to be the same as elsewhere too.

And on a more intangible level being middle-class and Irish had things to offer which being merely middle-class elsewhere did not.

Whatever the comparative strength of your religious feelings, often being Irish means to have a sort of heritage of philosophical certainty which can be taken largely for granted. Residual Catholicism tends, at the very least, to dull the sort of questionings about one's place in the universe and the value of a small success which might otherwise afflict one in the watches of the night. It tends, at the very least, to conceal the void. With its emphasis on an individual salvation in an after-life, to be secured by the observance of magical and propitiatory rites, it successfully occludes all the major questions about the ultimate worth and significance of one's activities or way of life. And since progressive Catholicism, having removed the restrictions on and abandoned the rules of conduct which afflicted older generations, tends to put more rather than less emphasis on mere observance of the minimum magical practices, it suits an emergent middle class, in a period of libertarian prosperity, almost better than any other religion that could be devised.

Besides prosperity, comparative ease of success and a large dollop of inherited philosophical certainty, the bulk of the members of the Irish middle class, have, or have had, at least up to now, other things going for them which lessened anxiety. They have in fact, whether they know it or not, much more of a monopoly of higher education than is the case elsewhere and a virtually exclusive right of entry into the professions. This means, of course, less competition, less class abrasions and less questioning of middle class values during the educational years (hence the general silliness of Irish student politics). And along with this easy demarcation of preserves there is the practical comfort of class domination, what M. Mitterand has called, speaking of his own country, the dictatorship of the bourgeoisie. So long as two essentially middle-class parties rule the roost, so long as working-class politics in southern Ireland is not class politics, so long as those who would tend to be either the most discontented or the most disruptive element in the urban proletariat (including those uprooted from the land) could be exported elsewhere – a day not yet, perhaps, done – the sort of anxiety which pervades the English middle class would be absent.

And finally, up to this point at least, there was a factor in the situation whose effects afforded deep re-assurance on psychological, material and philosophical levels all at once. Nothing is better guaranteed to dull questionings and anxieties of all descriptions than the belief that you have done well by the kids: that whatever sort of mess you personally are making of things, their future as interested, active, comparatively well-rewarded people is assured.

And so long as the education-job nexus, with its guarantee of automatically increased status and salaries for their offspring remained strong, those who had themselves enjoyed a period of middle-class expansionism could keep the most implacable of their anxieties, historical, philosophical and otherwise, quite easily at bay.

Now that the education-job nexus has broken down, and no amount of "growth" or "expansion" in terms of mere manufacturing output seems likely to restore it (more particularly if the manufacturers are not taxed) the results will be more far-reaching than anybody has yet grasped; but in the meantime the Irish middle-class psychology of the last quarter of a century or so survives.

That psychology, for the reasons given, was principally characterised by a deep, widespread and almost invulnerable complacency. Because of this complacency many otherwise inconceivable things were and are possible; because of it many questions simply do not arise; thought, on any but the most superficial levels, is, even among those whose business is thinking, almost non-existent; art is something smartish people feel they ought to know a little about. This complacency has, and will continue to have, many disguises, not least among them forms of social concern; and as it has survived the incursion of many shocking realities, it will doubtless survive a few more. But it must, in the nature of things, nevertheless have its term; and whatever else happens when that day comes, at least thought and art will then be regarded in a somewhat different light.

West of Clondalkin

IN THE last few decades large numbers of people from elsewhere in Ireland have chosen to take up residence in the city of Dublin, and it is common knowledge that most of the others would if they could. If, dear reader, you stroll, as the present writer occasionally strolls, along the production lines in Radio Eireann, the accents that will greet you (or not greet you, as the case may be) on all sides will be rural accents.

If you enter any of the hired and expensive warrens where the State's apparatchik are housed, the accents you will hear on the telephones in active control of your destinies, whether of high rank, and thus probably male, or of low, and therefore more likely to be female, will be indubitably rural. If you tread even the pathways of commerce, more particularly the larger bureaucracy sort of commerce, the dulcet tones of rurality will be everywhere to be heard. Fall into the clutches of a policeman: the same thing. Be refused a drink by a publican's assistant at twenty-five past two: for the most part *idem*. Board even a bus: ditto. And so on and so forth. The Irish people, in brief, have voted with their feet. The dwellers in the most beautiful of rural surroundings have deserted them for elsewhere. Those that did not have the option of the capital, the rural proletariat, went to Birmingham, Leeds, Bradford, *et al*; but those that had the requisite political pull, knowledge of typewriting or talent for passing examinations flocked into Dublin.

And yet a rural bias remains, and a prevalent rural nostalgia. The actual departure from Ballymacarbry and the slopes of Slieve Miskish was not accompanied by a movement of the heart. Far from it in fact. The rewards and comforts of the city having been accepted and its fleshpots tasted, the mental flight, as reflected in our art and literature, our songs and our imaginations, was in the reverse direction.

Right from the foundation of the State there was an assumption that though Dublin was growing and growing (at present it houses about a third of the population) the true matter of Ireland, the stuff of its life, both material and spiritual, lay behind it in the hinterland, at the end of the long road to Umeragh and points west. There were the true griddle cakes, the great footballers, the sharp grandmothers, the witty spailpíns of the schoolyard, the weighty speakers of the wise and kingly. More questionably perhaps, there were the characters whose reality was proven by word and gesture; there were the circumstances which truly reflected human nature; and there were the specifically poetic emotions. In the move to the city the touchstones had been lost.

Now, it is natural enough to feel these rather unoriginal things after a move to the city from rural parts. The songs of the city are frequently songs of green fields far away. And it is also natural to look back to childhood surroundings, childhood companions and the events of one's nonage as to the surroundings, companions and events of a golden age. (No matter that the present writer doesn't. There are ways in which he is an exception.) What the Irish people, and their representatives in art and literature seemed to feel, though, was more than this, for when the feeling was at its strongest there seemed to lie behind it an assumption that the actual circumstances of city life and the realities of the twentieth century were somehow illusory; that the day-to-day details of life in the city were not so important or so interesting as the day-to-day details of life in a more imaginary rural past; that the primitive was the true norm and the patently doomed and passing was the timeless; that rural reality, in short, was somehow more real than urban. And what was and is certainly unusual about the Irish situation would be the fact that the ones who benefitted most from the move to the city, the sharpish intelligentsia, the media men and the sophisticates (local brand of) should apparently feel this rural nostalgia most.

And the more rural the rurality apparently the better. When you got to the rock-bound coasts of the desolated west you encountered, so the story went, the realest thing of all. There, where people had almost vanished, what life did remain was somehow more passionate than the life of cities. Where dullness and monotony reigned supreme, the inhabitants were curiously more colourful than the people in Grafton Street. Even the shivering beasts which cropped the scant grass of the minutely apportioned fields led lives far richer and stranger than the duller beasts of Meath and County Dublin. And some of them could almost talk.

But the west was only the ultimate of the dream landscape. Even the small towns of north Munster and the midlands were invested with a glamour far, far exceeding their deserts. And as for the small towns of Kerry . . . the present writer remembers long conversations during which minute distinctions were drawn between the character and attainments of the inhabitants of various not very easily distinguishable places in which the connoisseurs would fear to spend (and had no intention of spending) more than a long week-end. And as with towns, so with counties. The forms of wassail and uninhibited romp distinctively on offer in each one were and are a constant topic of conversation among those who have no intention of enjoying more than an occasional subsidised motor journey over the borders on behalf of the media; while the comparative virtues of the people of various administrative areas are discussed in transit with a zeal of which human nature itself is scarcely worthy of being the object. For some reason the people of Clare often come in for especially high praise — the establishment has, of course, an annual outing to that county — and since the present writer has lived among the people of Clare he may be allowed to comment: they are a decent, careful people and though, like most of the rural Irish, over-devoted to small money dealings the morality of which they are inclined to carry into their dealings with the Almighty, they are quite conversable. In short, they are fine; but they do not sing with as high a note as the members of the Merriman Society make out.

Now, as has been said, a certain amount of nostalgia for lost roots is usual in a people in transition. The pastoral dream continues to be nourished in penthouse, tenement and suburb (less often in penthouse than in the other). The English have been gravely troubled by pastoral longings since the days of Wordsworth and William Blake; and the yearning for pastoral is certainly responsible for most of their distortions of literary judgement. Scarcely anywhere, though, can it have attained the depth and intensity (not to mention the sheer heights of fraudulence) which it has in the Free State in our time. Already present in the Protestant gentlefolk who created the Celtic Renaissance, it was echoed by the native writers of the nineteen-twenties (Cork men included: there is a recognisable old Cork version of pastoral) and by the painters whose works the new establishment delighted to possess. When broadcasting came along it received another big fillip, and the television has been moidered by it since the days of its inauguration. The present writer believes that backward-looking primitivism has been the principal cause of the failure of Free State nationalism to produce worthwhile results. Likewise he holds that it has been one of the principal causes of the failure of the language movement (the other was jobbery). And he is prepared to declare that the special slant given to the language movement and to the folk music thing by this kind of primitivism has made them the enemies of other kinds of cultural exploration and achievement in twentieth century Ireland.

He thinks furthermore that the root causes of its perpetuation lie in the guilts the new intelligentsia feel about their origins, their abandonments, their acceptances and (not least) their relationship with the city of Dublin and the Dublin working class — just as some of its origin lay in similar feelings on the part of the

Protestant gentlefolk of the Celtic Renaissance about themselves and the Irish people in general. He is a conservator (not to say a conservative) by nature and he is all for respecting our roots and origins. But he feels that there is a strong element of duplicity in what he has been describing: and he is utterly convinced that we have in Ireland more than enough duplicity.

Who's for Culture?

THE MOST Reverend Dr Eames, Church of Ireland Bishop of Derry and Raphoe, is reported as having attacked "the insensitivity of southern politicians" about the Northern question in a speech to the Church of Ireland Synod recently; and as having drawn attention "to the genuine fear of Northern Protestants that political unity would involve a sellout and domination of their political, cultural and religious life."

When I read this kind of thing my own first feeling is that in these sorts of times everybody should mind their language. Not more than a few hundred people — say at the outside about 700 — in this island, north and south, have a cultural life worth speaking of, and in loosely suggesting otherwise the Most Reverend Bishop is concealing or ignoring the tragic facts, which is not the sort of thing that Bishops should be up to, in these times or otherwise.

Having a picture of the Queen of England on your wall does not amount to having a culture, a separate culture or a cultural life. Speaking with a South Down accent (or a Derry or Raphoe accent) does not constitute having a cultural life. Marching twice a year behind penny whistles playing borrowed come-all-ye's in a tribal festival of hate and fear is not, in spite of all the pro-unionist sentimentality now going on, a cultural activity worthy of a civilised man's respect: indeed it is scarcely one worthy of his other than humorous indulgence. Wearing a bowler hat on occasions of ceremony or tribal importance is not a mark of culture, superior, inferior or otherwise. There are plenty of people in the south of Ireland who wear bowler hats on occasion and the bishop can take it from me that they are people of no culture at all.

Of course there is a broad, rather rubbishy anthropological sense in which everything you are or do constitutes a culture. Eating fish and chips rather than toast and caviare, supporting Manchester United rather than the Middlesex Cricket Club, watching Top of the Pops, going to work in a factory, behaving in certain recognisable ways at weddings, funerals and christenings all add up to a culture, provided sufficient numbers of other people do the same. In that sense the people of the Shankill Road, Ringsend and the Scotland Division of Liverpool all have a culture or a cultural life, and it is much the same culture or — for what it's worth — cultural life. In that sense going to Church of Ireland service, reading *Homes and Gardens* and eating tea and muffins at four o'clock in the afternoon is to be described as having a cultural life, or a separate cultural life, or a distinct and separate culture; and although there are still a few people in the south of Ireland who constitute, or who belong to or who have such a separate culture or cultural life (separate that is from other people here) if they are being trampled upon it is by the forces at large in the world in general, including economic forces, not by the volitional will of wicked or ambitious southern politicians.

In other words, if the bishop is talking in anthropological terms, what he is saying is, as near as makes no difference, meaningless. The cultural life of most people nowadays is a mixture of traditional and modern patterns of behaviour — the modern ones being, most of them, sadly enough, media-induced — in which the traditional ones are losing out to the modern. It varies from class to class; to some extent from occupation to occupation and, to some extent also, from age group to age group. It does not vary from north to south. The ancient farmer mumbling in the chimney corner about times gone by and the terrible, terrible things that are happening in the world is much the same fellow, north or south. So is the heir and inheritor stepping into his Mercedes to do a bit of social gin-drinking followed by you know what.

If in this restricted pseudo-scientific sense the cultural life of people is being dominated, it is being dominated, north and south, by forces far more sinister than southern politicians and, for the moment, largely outside the control of anybody in these parts.

It is true, of course that there is a shadowy borderland of sorts between what is meant by culture or cultural life in the anthropological sense and what is meant by either word or phrase when used by us laymen. Between having a culture or belonging to a culture (drinking lemon barley water, say, rather than coca cola) and being a cultured person in the sense of having some knowledge of the difference between synthetic cubism and analytic cubism there is a realm which, if one may say so without offence to anybody (what a hope!) may be inhabited by enthusiasts for the Irish language, saffron kilts and even more or less traditional forms of Irish music. The bishop may feel that, whatever their drinking or courting habits, and whether or not they have a cultural life, these people constitute a culture, that they have politicians fronting for them and that they are going to impose their fanatical will on him to the detriment of his continued ability to make himself understood in his native island, his preference for gaiters (if he has a preference for gaiters) and his freedom of musical choice.

Let him be assured. It would take a long time to explain to him the difference between the various forms of revivalism now extant. We would be a weary time at it if my own not so reverend self's mixture of feelings about some of the methods of revival and their connection with politics were to be the subject of our discourse today. But on the score of imposition Dr Eames may rest easy. The politicians down here have the enthusiasm for the language now gauged to a tenth; and they are for the most part now behaving in accordance with that measurement. If they had to swallow the north as well they would be that much less likely to impose it on anybody; and though there is a sense in which the folk-music thing has grown into a rather boring threat to other forms of cultural life, the politicians are not really clever enough to give a hoot about it one way or another.

They may, in a way, benefit from cultural deprivation; they may, therefore, be the gainers from the fact that swallowing pints in company with the music is the nearest approach to a cultural life that most people now have, but they are not so brilliant as to have been able to think it all up and exploit it — other people have done that.

No, the sad fact is, to cut a long story short, that in the seats of the mighty, north and south, there is not much interest in culture as you and I understand that word. In fact the British government sustains such cultural life as exists in the north with more hard cash than any government seems prepared to spend in the free Ireland of the south, and the problem is therefore likely to be vastly (but vastly) more one of neglect and continuing cold indifference rather than of any possible or foreseeable form of domination.

Since the cultural life of the two ends of the island is, in so far as it exists at all, the same thing; and since, for example, its modern literature is mostly in English and is largely a southern Protestant creation, it is hard to see how such domination as might keep the reverend gentleman awake at night could come about anyway. But in face of the attenuation, the hypocrisy and the neglect which are the hard facts of the matter, to speak of our politicians dominating anybody's cultural life is rubbish. Fanciful talk about political and religious domination is bad enough, but please let's leave culture out of it.

Material and Spiritual

THE FINE Gael Party has, through its dashing new leader, come out against materialism; and though it has not said which particular variety of spiritualism it feels should take its place, anybody in Ireland who reads the newspapers and has suffered several thousand condemnations of materialism in the course of an average lifetime could nearly supply the answer. It must be either the Christian religion or selfless service to the community.

The first thing to be said about condemnations of materialism, though, is that they sit ill on the lips of those who have more than anybody else, even if it is only fractionally more. Condemnations of materialism ought to be the prerogative of gurus who sleep on planks with their ribs showing or saints who grub for periwinkles by the shore. They do not sound fitting even on the lips of what used to be called the comfortably circumstanced or the moderately well-off; and unless, like the founder of the Christian religion, you are prepared to take to the roads and ditches you had best perhaps keep quiet about your preference for other-worldly values.

The second thing to be said of course is that materialism is the least of man's problems; and that it is a sort of treason to his courage and his resource — a sort of blasphemy against man himself — to say otherwise. Competitiveness may be a problem. Greed may be a problem. The thought that commerce and competition, (even competition between east and west, socialist and non-socialist countries) fills the world with useless and pernicious things while others are hard to come by, may keep one awake at night.

But material wealth, even of the most obnoxious kind, is the fruit of man's endless curiosity, his ingenuity and his labour, and should be respected as such; and of course all condemnations of materialism per se, even those directed specifically at those segments of society which are most evidently guilty of mere material greed, wastage and display (the famous Fianna Fáil gombeen men, etc.) are mere hot air unless accompanied by an exact and lucid spelling out of what you desire in the way of an alternative, and whether it be prayer, sacrifice, meditation, redistribution, re-allocation or control.

If Dr Fitzgerald wants a nation of saints and ascetics, clod-hoppers and comely maidens a la Dev's old pipedream he should say so. He should also say whether he proposes to start the process of material divestment at the top and work down or, like the people who call for restraint and sacrifice in the national interest, at the bottom; how he proposes to bring it about; and in the absence of any philosophic certitude about the purpose of human life on this planet after we have all rendered up the television set, what good is it. (It would seem to the present writer that once you accept the free flow of capital and the freedom of commerce to create needs, even pernicious needs, and satisfy them, you become ultimately just as materialistic as the Californians, no more and no less. It may be an unhappy, a savage, or even a guilt-laden materialism; but materialism it will be just the same).

There is no doubt of course that our society has problems in relation to the material basis of existence and that they are somewhat different from the sort our ancestors or the eskimos or the bushmen had. Apart from the fact that some people don't have enough of it (even those who have coloured television sets frequently have inadequate housing) there has been another industrial revolution which means that the machines now do much more of the work than they ever did before and with the intervention of less people. The machines, in other words, are now actively disemploying the human work-force; and although those already in employment have means of staying there by hook or by crook, the merciless effect is now quite clearly seen in the superfluousness of those arriving on the labour market for the first time.

This means that capital investment will no longer produce employment, though it may produce a boom of sorts. Indeed it is likely that the boom we are in for (the boom already upon us) will, whatever Martin O'Donoghue does, be accompanied by steady unemployment; and that probably not even those ancient panaceas (ancient but never tried so to speak) the shorter working week, longer holidays and earlier redundancies, would save us from the situation — quite different from the sixties — of having a boom at the top with all the vulgarity and crude display that goes with it and a mass of people (mostly young people) kept barely at the subsistence level below. The fact that they will have little or no purchasing power will make little difference since home demand will have little to do with the matter and the industry we do get will be geared for export.

For Britain, Shirley Williams proposed at Blackpool a two-tier system in which the top tier consisted of a handful of major industries with high productivity and low manpower and the lower of the sort of services and industries which are important to a civilised community. The top tier would produce the wealth and the lower one employ the people, hopefully in ways that gave them job satisfaction and a sense of purpose.

It is an intelligent woman's fantasy, of course, unless Mrs Williams means to bring socialism about first; for as it stands the British system is not flexible enough and government control of investment is not sufficiently far-reaching or daringly enough employed to create the transformation needed; but it shows a recognition of the fact that the business of industry is to create wealth, not jobs, and that the problem for those in charge ought to be how to distribute the wealth produced.

Behind it all, of course, lies the problem of human purpose. Even if it was true that we all lived in a stuffed and sated materialist society that problem would not go away. Indeed it might be said that it would only then arise. Then man might decide that something more was needed than more and more goods and gadgets; and the ultimate role of the artist might be seen for what it is. Hasten the day.

God and Mammon

THE GREAT Russian scientist, Ivan Petrovich Pavlov (1849-1936), who pioneered the study of conditioned reflexes and won the Nobel Prize for his work on the digestive glands, succeeded in reducing rats, dogs and other animals to neurotic wrecks by the use of contradictory stimuli. One day of flashing red light meant food; the next day it meant an electric shock. You saw the light flash, you ran eagerly through the little tunnel, pushed open the little door with your little snout and the next thing you knew you had got an exceedingly nasty shock in the same proboscis. Then he began the treacherous process of accustoming ("conditioning") you to believe that the flashing red light meant food again; and so on until you were a sad case and ready for one of Mr Pavlov's psychiatrist friends to get to work on.

If anyone paid any attention to them, it would be the same with these two words "growth" and "materialism". Materialism, according to the Supreme Pontiff, the bishops, the leader of the Fine Gael Party, Mr Richie Ryan and other politicians, is a bad thing. Growth, according to most of the politicians and economists, including the leader of the Fine Gael Party and Mr Richie Ryan, is a good thing.

Materialism is motor bikes for young fellows out in Finglas and Ballyfermot. It is transistors, tape recorders and electronic gear of all sorts for all and sundry. It is an Audi for him and a Mazda for her. It is washing machines, deep-freezes, Leicas and Practikas. It is unguents and creams for comely maidens and hair-dryers for manly youths. It is coloured television sets. It is gin-soaked Continental holidays on sun soaked beaches. It is buying wine for indifferent beauties in expensive night spots. It is getting into debt with the Credit Union, the bank manager and whoever else is clever or stupid enough to lend you money. It is the little of what you fancy that you mistakenly believe will do you good. It is the high road to Hell.

The trouble is that growth is all these things too only more so. If materialism is investing in an Audi to impress the little ladies of Leeson Street, growth is buying and eventually crashing a Mercedes to do the same. If materialism is such a blinder in Benidorm that sun and sea, indoors and out, night and day, balcony and bedroom are all one indistinguishable haze, growth is going off to repeat the performance three more times in the same year.

If materialism is imbibing the television programme 'Dallas' in full colour on Tuesdays and Thursdays, growth is buying a telerecorder so that you can watch it every night in the week and re-run it at three o'clock in the morning if the impulse overcomes you. If materialism is borrowing two thousand quid from the bank manager on pretence of a business opportunity when your actual intention is to take off for Singapore and Hong Kong, growth is double that sum and a bash in Las Vegas from which you may never recover.

Yet the curious thing is that with the possible exceptions of the Lords Bishops and the Supreme Pontiff, the very same people who condemn the one recommend the other: nay, they declare it is essential and that without it we are doomed and lost. Garret Fitzgerald, who belongs to the spiritual tradition of Fine Gael and its predecessor, the old Cumann na nGaedheal party, is never done speaking sad words about materialism. Yet his eyes light up and something of the buoyant optimism of the halcyon old Keynesian days comes back into his voice when he speaks about growth. Mr George Colley and Dr Martin O'Donoghue, who belong to the slightly less spiritual tradition of Fianna Fáil, have deplored materialism, especially the materialism of trade union members, in tones more of sorrow than of anger. Yet they warn us daily that without growth the game is up and our goose is cooked; and you can bet your last button they are both aware by now that without growth their game is up and their goose is (politically) cooked.

Of course, there is national growth and international growth. One might believe that they want us to grow like mad here without importing any Audis or drinking any vodkas in Torremolinos at all, just putting the money in the bank like Cumann na nGaedheal subscribers used once to do. No such thing. In this respect as in others they are at one with Mr Carter and Herr Schmidt; and when Mr Carter, Herr Schmidt, the Japs and the bankers get together at one of those conferences in Tokyo or the Bahamas, the first thing they all agree on is that growth is one, holy, and, if not Roman, then truly indivisible.

Growth, they are agreed, is the most international thing of all, more international even than the British thoroughbred or the rules of Association Football. It is international or it is nothing: and in fact the only politician in the whole capitalist world who is saying otherwise at the moment is our old friend Mr Tony Benn. He believes, and good luck to him, that there is a sort of British growth that could be brought about on his own right little tight little island by telling the Japanese and the IFM and even the gnomes of Zurich to stuff their international recipes for recovery up their jerseys.

Of course the difference between Tony Benn and the others is that the possible collapse of the system does not keep him awake at night. What the others all know is that for the continuance of the system, growth, more growth, and then more growth again, is the first and last essential.

Every evidence of a setback to growth — that is, to widespread and continuing addiction to and dependence on the material products of manufacture, no matter how preposterous, corrupting or useless they may be — gives them the heebie-jeebies. Every time a continuing threat of unmanageable inflation forces them, as in the United States at the moment, to cut back on credit and stop ordinary people getting into debt up to the oxters for more and more gear and paraphernalia, more and more debauchery and luxury, they feel that at last the old German's prognostications may be coming true and the next thing will be ruin, revolution, rapine and collapse.

And really, my dears, it is asking too much to believe that the Lords Bishops and even the Supreme Pontiff don't know the same thing. Conspicuous waste, conspicuous expenditure on more or less enjoyable or pernicious gadgets and good times are, in economic terms, and in our system, and in spite of all the talk about the oil shortage, virtues. Of course, not everybody is allowed or expected to share in them to the same degree; but when some people, who may not even be sharing in them to any very great degree at all, demand a little more goodies, or even a few necessities to the detriment of somebody's or some "sector's" immediate profits, the warnings against and the denunciations of materialism are frequently redoubled.

To be fair to some of the warners, I believe that in a muddled sort of way — philosophically at least — they mean what they say. Speaking for myself, I even know what they mean, but would one of them preach us a sermon in which the spiritual forebodings and the hard economic facts of the matter are reconciled? Might I suggest Mr Richie Ryan, who is an Old Christian Brothers' boy and has perhaps a fractionally greater grasp of economics than Mr George Colley, for the job?

Some More Equal Than Others

BEFORE AMERICAN Independence year finally vanishes, let us examine the proposition that all men are created equal. It is, of course, in the sense in which it is often cited and argued over, preposterous. Although the sameness of human beings is a source of constant amazement to the observer, in many ways that matter greatly, and in some that don't, human beings differ enormously from each other, being equal neither in intelligence, strength, courage, eloquence, beauty, cunning or anything else. What the authors of the Declaration of Independence meant, however, was that men had a right to be regarded as equal by the law or by society. "All men are created equal," they said, "and are endowed by God with certain inalienable rights." But this is a proposition even more ludicrous than the claim that they are equal in their innate capacities. There are no "rights" anterior to human law and human organisation and only the supreme philosophical arrogance of 18th century Deism allowed Jefferson and the others to allege that there were. There may or may not be rights temporarily enshrined in the law of the society in which you happen to live and enforceable by that law, but other rights are hokum, philosophical, theological or otherwise. When the rights you foolishly believe you have are abrogated the only appeal is to force, though other men may be moved by their human sense of justice to use that force on your behalf.

And as far as innate capacity is concerned there is no reason to mourn the inequality of man. It is perhaps a pity that not everybody can climb the Matterhorn, run the mile in three minutes fifty seconds or write a novel like Marcel Proust's but for one thing not everybody wants to; and in the meantime it is much more sensible to be glad that some people can. For while the greatest amongst us paint pictures that open the eyes of the rest, isolate the causes of disease or improve our use of language, the capacity of the whole human race is extended and its chances of survival increased.

Nor is it likely that most of the exceptional things which are worth doing would continue to get done if those who did them were not rewarded or honoured in some way. The feeling of being exceptional which most exceptional people have is closely allied with the desire to be recognised as such. Glory, honour, fame are words misused almost beyond redemption; and the facts of such glory, honour or fame as can be said to exist in our society are not, on the whole, pretty ones. Most of the fame that is on offer must be deeply suspect to people with their wits about them; and honours lists are a joke; but nevertheless the wish to have one's talents recognised and one's achievement esteemed goes very deep in the human make-up, and if the hope of recognition and esteem were removed entirely tomorrow the world would be in poor case.

It is true that the sense of vocation – a word, like so much else, mis-appropriated by the Church in Ireland – would remain; as would curiosity, joy in the exercise of superior skills, the determination to do and to demonstrate and even the altruistic wish (rather different from a sense of vocation) to improve the lot of humanity in general or assist the evolutionary process on its way. But the wish for true fame and true glory as these words have been interpreted by mankind in other societies than ours and before the advertiser came along to muddy all the waters, goes so deep that it is probable that mankind's achievements would be considerably the less if it were not felt to be somewhere, somehow and at some time, even if only posthumously, on offer. Nor is the desire to be distinguished in the eyes of one's fellows and have one's attractions, such as they may be, thereby enhanced an ignoble one. Far from it. To the wild and secret extravagances of the heart, or, to put it another way, to the delusion that genuine achievement will impress the members of the opposite, or any sex, we owe a great deal.

But all this is quite different from saying that true human achievement is based on acquisitiveness or the power urge. There may have been a time, and it may have occupied a long span of human history, when the acquisitive man served the purposes of the race, or at least the tribe. Clad in his armour or wielding his spear he may have afforded protection, provoked emulation, and even improved the genetic possibilities by getting hold of the most desirable girls. One says "may have" because there are at least two schools of thought. Even the luminaries of the new "science" of ethology, who claim that all human behaviour is governed by patterns established in the pre-human, higher primate phase, do not list possessions (other than control and domination over a few females) as among the rewards of exceptional primate behaviour; while pre-historians in general are agreed that in the hunting society of the paleolithic era (a span which was 20 times as long as all the subseqeunt ones put together) possession – or even power – played a very small part in human affairs. The best hunter got the best cut. On matters within his provenance, though certainly not on those, such as art, without it, his advice was listened to; and that was all.

And if it was ever the case that humanity was spurred to achievement by acquisitiveness and the power urge, it is so no longer. The "acquisitive man" contributes little or nothing to our worthwhile store of scientific knowledge for the simple reason that most worthwhile scientific discoveries are made by people who are comparatively careless of the rewards to be had. He writes not our best but our worst plays and novels. He paints hardly any pictures nowadays for the simple reason that there is not much market for the sort of pictures he painted during the 19th century; and he writes no poems whatever for the reason that there is no market whatever for poems.

And in all other areas he is a disaster. In those activities verging on art where commercial considerations are important – in the design of buildings, the making of television programmes and the production of films – the results are worse than if they played no part. Commerce, as commerce, more and more patently fails to deliver the goods every day in the week, and its vaunted ability to do so is more and more clearly seen to be dependent on exploitation and a criminal misuse of the world's resources. The "higher executives" who are "attracted into management" by "adequate incentives" cannot even keep the number 3 bus running on Christmas Eve. At the top level in all the larger corporations people spend more time figuring out tax dodges and worrying about the social complications the famous incentives involve them in than they do in improving the quality of the service; while even the bureaucratic inefficiency and slackness which by all accounts effect all levels of life in the Soviet Union have far more to do with the presence of incentives and rewards and the fear of losing them than they have to do with their absence.

Furthermore most men and women who are true achievers would be happier if reward differentials were abolished completely; if everybody was rewarded equally for any work which was considered worth doing; and was given the means to get on with the job. Perhaps the greatest single crime of commercially governed society is the misuse, wastage and ignorance of the talents and capacities of genius which are inherent in it. For this at the moment, as well as for the rapacities of the profit motive, we are paying an evolutionary price too high to contemplate. The other night on the television Hugh Mac Diarmuid said he was a communist because he was an elitist. Like everybody else who has given thought to the subject he knows that true fame could only exist in a society from which the caricatures of honour and glory produced by commerce had been banished. Only in such could real achievement shine forth other than as a good deed in a naughty world; and only in such could the blessed inequalities of men and women come to full fruition.

Public Enterprise

THAT THE existing State corporations are no advertisement for the extension of State control over anything is a fact so blindingly obvious to your man in the street that he no longer expresses it by way of a direct proposition, confining himself to such gnomic queries as; "What do you expect from that shower?" or; "Is there e'er a one of them ever did a day's work in their lives?"

But his objections are not, be it noted, based on *a priori* theories about State control. Unlike Mrs Thatcher or Sir Keith Joseph across the Channel, he does not believe that if you hand over, say, the raising and marketing of chickens or the manufacture and distribution of hair oil to the State, we will all wind up in a concentration camp. He is not deeply committed to the philosophy of private enterprise; and his conclusions are based on everyday pragmatical rather than merely theoretical grounds. The organisations in question either do not provide the service he requires, they provide it at too great a cost, or they ally the provision with extreme, unwarrantable and most unbrookable rudeness, ill-grace and insults to his dignity.

Sometimes, it is true, he does express an opinion on the general question of private enterprise versus State control. He believes, in general, that a bit of competition would liven them all up; that they should be made to meet the public on equal terms; or that if the whole shebang was handed over to someone who knew anything about how to run it he would not be left standing in the rain so often and might occasionally find a public telephone which works.

And in this he might well be right. Private enterprise (by which is often meant corporations larger than any conceivable State corporation this country might have) does occasionally perform miracles. It does deliver the goods. It is responsive to public demand. And it does try to please.

The trouble is that the goods it delivers are not always the right goods, and it will deliver no goods at all unless it is profitable to do so. It is not only responsive to public demand, but it creates demand; and the demand is often for useless, pernicious or ugly things which people only want because it brainwashes them into doing so.

From which it follows that in the matter of total, over-all allocation of our resources, private enterprise is often the enemy of sense and reason. In the overall picture it is lazy, wasteful, inefficient and corruptive. It is not interested in making us any healthier, or happier, or able to use such leisure as we may have in more rewarding ways. It will not, unless as part of a larger package, on which it will try to renege, provide unprofitable services of any kind. And it will certainly not solve the problem of putting us all to work or, which is far more important, supporting us all while we do useful or rewarding or enjoyable things.

But these are theoretical considerations, and to urge them on someone left standing in D'Olier Street for three-quarters of an hour on a bitter July evening, or reduced to tears and frenzy by an attempt to find a public telephone box which had a telephone in it, might be to invite sudden death. As far as the man in the street is concerned, state enterprise as he experiences it is largely a washout; and it is impossible not to sympathise with his point of view.

The ESB, for example, is an organisation whose general ineptitude is matched only by its extreme contempt for the public which it purports to serve. To have any dealings whatever with it is a bitter and chastening experience. Not long ago it was found by the Prices Commission to be employing a number of supernumeraries who had no connection whatever with the supply of electricity except that their unexplained presence in the organisation inflated its price; and whether this is the reason or not, its rates are the highest in Europe.

To attempt to add anything to what is daily said about the telephone service (or, more precisely, the lack of one) would be to strain the limits of prose and invite prosecution for obscenity. The workings of CIE are a daily torment and a conundrum to all who are dependent on it. The state airline survives because it charges a preposterous fare for the short journey to the sister island which thousands of exiles and others must make several times a year. And about the organisation out in Donnybrook which supplies you with radio and television, perhaps the least said the soonest mended.

But one must insist that to say all this is not really to pass a judgement on the true possibilities of communal ownership of anything. Our semi-states are all bureaucracies which reflect the characteristic of the larger bureaucracy which gave them birth. It may or may not be true that the people who run them do not do as much work as our man in the street does himself: what is certain is that the work which is done is performed in an atmosphere of timorousness, pusillanimity and deference to the system which is bound to be detrimental to real effort, originality and achievement.

It may be that we in Ireland turned originally to bureaucracy only through a version of the deadly attraction of opposites, as a man with strong sexual urges will enter a monastery or nations composed almost entirely of drunkards will pass prohibition laws. But what is certain is that we turned to it also in response to temptations held out to individuals (often the brightest individuals) via the examination system by those whose interest was to subvert and tame the national genius rather than to allow it free rein; and the results have been obvious ever since.

Yet the people at the top of the semi-states, when not bureaucrats pure and simple, are very often the sort of people who are hostile to the whole underlying ethic of communal ownership and endeavour. Some of these whizz-kids are refugees from private enterprise. Some of them well-advertised failures in several spheres at once. They are the sort of fellows who believe that the more subordinates a man has and the more he makes them hop, the more his power and efficiency is proved. The results are again obvious.

For these reasons it is fairly generally true that the people who actually do the basic job are the people who rescue the organisations concerned from even greater chaos. The average Dublin bus-driver performs quiet miracles of efficiency and endeavour every day. The average conductor is a model of courtesy and helpfulness in his dealings with the public. On balance, the workers tend to believe more wholeheartedly in public ownership and control than do the bureaucrats. On balance the workers do the job; the bureaucrats do not.

The answer may therefore lie in an extension of worker control; but whatever the answer, there is no use denying that there is not currently a problem. Ultimately the problem involves our conception of the state; what exactly "state ownership" means; and how long, even in a possible future in which there is no private enterprise at all, state ownership should last. The general anti-utopian bias of the Left inhibits discussion of these problems even on the Left; but in the meantime, confronted as he is with CIE, the ESB and the other giants of initialdom, the man in the street has his own opinion. He has seen state control in action; and he does not thank you for suggesting any more of it.

Larning or Larupping?

A YOUNG doctor was recently reported in the newspapers as having torn up his scrip or parchment, or whatever it is doctors get, in protest against the examination system. His point was a simple one. The examination situation is never reproduced in later life and is therefore not a fair test of anybody's abilities.

Now, medicine aside for the moment, examinations and all that surrounds them are such a strange, traumatic thing in Irish life that one approaches the subject with a certain amount of trepidation. In the reverence for the examination, one feels, lies, if anywhere, the heart of the matter, the key to those mysterious aspects of the Irish character which have baffled friend and foe alike. Whatever happened to the race, whatever the explanation of the contrast between the gay, anarchic Irishman of legend and the permanent and pensionable fellow he apparently all too easily becomes, the answer may lie in the eagerness with which he submits himself from an early age to a series of scholastic examinations, the reverence with which he regards the results, the almost religious awe with which he accepts them as a life-long arbiter of ability, character and consequent happiness.

How did these attitudes come about? Was it, one wonders, some ferocious con-trick worked by the British in the last, apparently mellow years of their rule? Paddy had been known from the earliest times to have a natural reverence for knowledge. His proudest boast about his island was that it had once been inhabited almost entirely by scholars and saints of European repute. Even in the dark days, whether cleanliness was next to godliness or not, latinity certainly seemed to him to go cheek by jowl with divinity. Mere literacy he accounted a state of bliss; learning augured blessedness beyond compare. Apart from anything else a measure of one or the other was a licence for otherwise reprehensible habits of idleness, lechery and drunkenness, and for this reason a reputation for either was eagerly sought.

Would it not be possible, Lord Macaulay or somebody else may have thought, to harness this force, to ally it with the desire for respectability, the fear of the unknown and the burning desire to get one's hands on public money which were also recognised as national characteristics? Given the co-operation of Maynooth and the religious orders, it might; indeed, not to put too fine a tooth on it, it was; and the result was the examination system and all its attendant evils, such as the civil service as we know it.

Now, that the preparation of aspirants for, and the subsequent passing of, examinations have nothing whatever to do with anything that might be remotely described as education is a fact so obvious that even such giant intellects and well-known educationalists as Basedow, Dewey, Fellenberg, Herbert Horace Mann, Pestalozzi, Ratichius and Bertrand Russell have been able to grasp it. One would have thought it needed no labouring. Education has to do with receptiveness all right but it also has to do with openness, growth, understanding, freedom and truth to oneself. It can no more be conducted without the joyous co-operation of the to-be-educated than a race can be run without runners. If it fails to elicit from even the most moon-faced that holy joy in the voluntary acquisition of knowledge without any care for its use which is high among humanity's redeeming traits, it has failed of its purposes.

But for these primary and delightful impulses the examination system substitutes all sorts of degraded and degrading ones. The meanest is a fear of the future. Into the minds of adolescents, where, as far as the acquisition of knowledge if nothing else is concerned, a spirit of *carpe diem* should rule the day, the examination system obtrudes a vision of a fearful future in the rainswept home county with only childhood companions for company and childhood sweethearts for mates, far from the mad delights of O'Connell Street, automatic promotion through various grades, public money and pensions. Instead of a spirit of free enquiry it encourages a reverence for received opinion, assimilable and very likely inaccurate facts. Instead of making it clear to all at the outset that boldness and originality are at the very least their own reward, it encourages the candidate to believe that the safe thing is the right thing and will be so for ever and ever amen. For a delight in the dispensation which ordains that there is so much to learn and that so much of it is entrancing, which makes human knowledge a carnival where everybody may ultimately find the one side-show that really displays wonders, it substitutes a belief that all reading, enquiry, discussion and assimilation not directed towards the particular end of pleasing the examiners is idleness, villainy and dissipation. And if you seek its monuments, look about you.

But, it might be argued, the examination system at least provides the authorities with a workable method of ascertaining which among many worthy candidates for honours are the most deserving ones; it sorts out for the rest of us the number (and it is large) which we ought to support in later life through the medium of taxation, whether in the groves of academe, in the service of government or in the national television station.

The short answer to this argument is that a simple lottery system, such as (I understand from the learned works of the late Mr Ernest Bramah) was operated in ancient China, would probably do the job just as well, and in any event could scarcely do it worse. A somewhat longer reply would be to the effect that examinations are primarily tests of memory, handwriting, powers of instant concentration and low cunning, and that these attributes are not necessarily those which distinguish the men and women who make genuine advances in any sphere of human activity. It might further be argued, as the young doctor did in effect, that the examination system presupposes that the candidate will sooner or later be marooned on a desert island, far from reference libraries, records and the converse and advice of colleagues; that on this barren atoll he will be confronted with the supreme crisis of his career, and that he will have to produce the answers within one hour and fifty minutes flat.

The doctor was right. An ability to pass examinations is no guide to subsequent distinction or even competence in any human activity. I go further. A facility for the passing of examinations is almost always the mark of the not quite first rate, the talented mediocrity who by and large likes things as they are. Lord Macaulay himself, we are told, failed to obtain a high degree at Trinity College Cambridge owing to his weakness in mathematics, a compulsory subject.

A Time to Rejoice in

THE RELIGION of the ancient Celtic inhabitants of this island was magical and propitiatory. You engaged in certain ritual observances and attended certain sacrifices in order to induce the gods to grant you certain favours, in the hope that they would ignore your transgressions and forgive you your impieties, or simply to ward off disaster and bad luck. The moral content of Celtic belief was small or non-existent. Religion to those ancient peoples was a means of establishing and maintaining cordial relations with the supernatural powers, big and small, local and supra-local, that ruled the world. And so also it was to the majority of the Irish of more recent times, even though they called themselves Christian.

So it may even, in spite of everything, be to the present day. Up to fairly recent times anyway, the magical and propitiatory aspect of Irish Catholicism far outweighed the moral. You did the Nine Fridays or went to Lough Derg or said a special decade of the rosary in order to get a husband, so that the son up in Dublin would pass his exams, to stop the head of the household drinking, or simply to ward off any of the multitudinous misfortunes with which human life is attended. And you were encouraged by the experts to believe that there would be a special magic exercised in your favour or that the law of cause and effect would somehow be bent if the ritual observances in which you engaged were fervent or frequent enough.

It is true that there was a greater moral content to Irish Catholicism than there (apparently) was to the ancient Celtic corpus of belief. As well as positive observances in the sphere of ritual, there were many negative injunctions and prohibitions in the realm of conduct, as well as a few taboos. These mainly related to sex and property and they ran so closely parallel to what might be called the respectability consensus of southern Irish society as to be more or less the same thing. There was of course some positive emphasis on helping or loving your neighbour through contribution to institutionalised charity; but in general a respectable man who obeyed all the laws of the State, was sexually abstinent except within the bounds of marriage and kept a civil tongue in his head when speaking of his neighbours, who was a member of a sodality and enthusiastic in his ritual observances, was what was called a good Catholic. If he was notorious for the frequency of his attendance at various rituals he was a very good Catholic.

Now it will be obvious to an observer of human nature that a society in which such a religion, so nearly synonymous with mere respectability, commanded the allegiance of the majority, was likely, of its nature to be a fairly hypocritical one. It was also likely to be of its nature, narrow, repressive, puritanical and cruel to the transgressor. And since greed and avarice, provided their manifestations were within the law, were not condemned (because the accumulation of wealth was a proof of respectability, in fact positively encouraged) it would also be, in any meaningful sense of the word, materialistic, its materialism being masked or disguised only by the despair, the apathy, or the resignation to their lot of large sections of the populace, urban and rural. And it might as well be said at this point that it was all these things and more.

The historical excursus is being made because when appeals are directed at us to return to traditional values we ought to be clear in our heads what those traditional values were. The traditional values and attitudes among which most of us were brought up were poor values and poor attitudes: fear of the supernatural, fear of hell-fire, fear of the neighbours, all at once: repression, joylessness, abnegation, even though the truth was that people refused to be repressed or to take quite such an abnegatory attitude to the fun they might have together as the spiritual authorities would have liked.

When His Holiness says in solemn condemnation before a vast concourse that; "Everybody wants a full freedom in all the areas of human behaviour and new models of morality are being proposed in the name of would-be freedom", it is important to be clear where we stand. And when he condemns as materialistic those who, now that "prosperity and affluence" are beginning to be available to them, "assume they have a right to all that prosperity can bring" it is important to be even clearer.

It is true that because respectability was such a power in the land, because the supernatural sanction, in particular the fear of hell-fire, was available as a weapon to Church and State alike, and because even the naturally lawless were curbed in ways that are no longer possible, there was a greater apparent safety for the person, and, in so far as it matters, a greater protection for property, in the world governed by those values than there is today, facts which mean that conservative appeals for a return to those values fall on very ready ears.

But there was also, let us remember, an amount of violence against the person which our spiritual pastors either ignored, approved, encouraged, or practised: violence in the schoolroom, violence in the home, violence against children, violence against women; and above all, perhaps, there was a constant and unremitting psychic violence against the body the effects of which can not be measured. And however slowly, and amid whatever confusions, much of that sort of violence is, in the world in which "everybody wants a full freedom", on the way out. Further, as far as material wealth or "property" was concerned, there was a positive deprivation of the many by the few, a cornering of comforts and necessities by legal means which amounted to robbery on a scale far greater than that suffered even by the many victims of criminal robbery today. That, let us hope, is on the way out too.

And so let us reflect that returning to the traditional values and the simple faith of our forefathers may not be such a rosy option as it looks, may not be just a question of the joys of congregation and consensus, of keeping the streets safe and the families together in some sort of patched-up harmony. Like it or not like it, one of the great movements of our time is the desire of everybody for "a full freedom in all the areas of human behaviour" and one of its great tasks the proposing of "new models of morality . . . in the name of would-be freedom". That the stage of evolution we are passing through has its pains and its difficulties, its traumas and its shocks we all know. Some people seem to need reminding that it has also, to put it mildly, its nobilities and its joys; but a clearer memory of what in fact went before, of what in fact simple faith and simple piety amounted to, may in any case make the shocks and the traumas easier to bear.

What Next?

AFTER THE Pope had been and gone, using the sky as his medium to beautiful effect, there was a good deal of rather comical thrashing around among those who had hoped to translate his visit into practical terms, visible or tangible to all. What, they asked us, sometimes in large capitals, did it all mean? What should we do next? How could we prove we meant it all?

Of course those nutty, or far out, or passionate or idealistic enough to hope for a Christian transformation of society were bound to be disappointed: maybe from the moment His Holiness first came down out of the sky and inspected a guard of honour of men armed with murderous weapons.

To those who have actually taken the trouble to read what Jesus said, the thing is quite clear; and to those who have any grasp of what our society is all about, quite clearly impossible. In a Christian society there would be neither prisons nor prisoners, judges nor gaolers. The whole apparatus of punishment and retaliation, of mutual protection against evil-doers by the use of superior force even (supposing that is what it is all about) would have to come to an end. The position of the judge, and the assumptions behind the robes and ermine, are as immoral and repugnant to Jesus as are the crimes of any criminal whatever. Even the judicial ritual which involves the taking of an oath in court of law is clearly forbidden by Matthew 5.33-37.

Of course, I am well aware that there are those who say that Christ was not talking about the transformation of society at all. Using the text about giving unto Caesar the things that are Caesar's (Matthew 22.21) and to God the things that are God's they insist that the message was all about private behaviour. I am also aware (as doubtless Herbert McCabe can confirm) that there is now a redoubtable and respectable building up of theological opinion to the effect that he really was talking about the Kingdom of God on Earth and that he would have been extremely disappointed to find that it had not come about after two thousand years. But even supposing private behaviour to have been what it was all about, expecting any sort of a large scale transformation on the part of individuals in our society is nonsense, and it founders for the most part on the same rocks as does the expectation of a specifically and overtly societal transformation: the rocks of greed, ambition, property-owning and power-seeking first and foremost, but also, on a humbler level, perhaps more applicable to most people's lives, those of mere fear, insecurity, worry and the expectation that when you are old you will be treated as a nuisance and a burden.

For if there were a large scale Christian transformation of our society, few people would make it the main business of their lives to secure a permanent and pensionable job; large numbers would not go to work in the morning at all; the rich who had been transformed by the Christian message would begin to liquidate their assets and give away their money to the poor, thereby causing a stock market crash, a run on the banks and the collapse of property values; hardly anybody would prosecute anybody else for debt (in the Authorised Version the Lord's Prayer as given by Matthew says "forgive us our debts as we forgive our debtors" with no vague nonsense about trespasses and trespassers at all); the converted when asked for a loan by a friend or even an acquaintance would immediately out with the readies or the cheque-book; no one who called himself a Christian would subscribe to a pension fund or even have any savings; and those of a stricter or more fervent disposition would begin to invite the homeless to share their houses, if they did not actually abandon them and take to the roads and ditches themselves. (Matthew 6.25 et sequentia, Luke 12.22 et sequentia and many other texts).

Nor, in spite of all that is said in his name, would family life or family loyalties be the gainers from any widescale conversion to Christianity in Ireland or elsewhere. Like almost all men who have a strong and urgent sense of vocation, Jesus regarded marriage, the family and the rearing of children as a trap. Like many who have a strong sense of the brotherhood of man and a clear realisation of the evil that we are all involved in so long as that brotherhood is not acknowledged, he regarded yielding to the more immediate claims of the family as a sort of treason to the larger loyalty. He would certainly have had no truck with those who pretend that mere self-aggrandisement through the education and advancement of one's children is in some way a fulfilment of his message; and he would have been appalled by any preacher who said in his name that the principal manifestations of our love for each other should be within the family circle. He thought the common notion of marriage as a bond which lasts through all eternity ridiculous. He treated his mother with impatience and discourtesy when he felt she was interrupting the work he had to do in the world; and he disowned his other relatives (perhaps his very brothers and sisters) in public in the rudest and most offhand manner.

The truth is that Jesus Christ was a classical anarchist and, whether or not he desired an immediate transformation of society along anarchist lines, he enjoined the kind of anarchism on his followers which, if they were sufficiently numerous, would bring it about. For the fact that they are not sufficiently numerous anywhere to make any change in things, the powers of this world, including all governments, finance houses, banks and large religious organisations can give devout thanks to whatever gods they believe in.

Of course there are those who hold that if we work through the gradual transformation and reorganisation of society — the word gradual not so much excluding those dramatic *bouleversements* which we call revolution as indicating the sort of toil-filled but nonetheless vision-inspired process which would have to come afterwards — we will achieve a state of things in which, to use the words of the Christian anarchist poet David Gascoyne, one could simultaneously "live one's own life and man's", taking no thought for the morrow, growing into vocational forgetfulness of the self as naturally as do the lilies of the field or the ravens of the sky, giving love for its own sake and not as a form of mutual insurance. How long, oh Lord, how long?

Stasis under the Crown

MR COSGRAVE will be in London today, talking to the British Prime Minister. The talks will occur on the heels of an easily foreseeable collapse of any prospect of agreement at the futile second Convention, but we must not expect anything very startling to emerge from the talks either. Mr Cosgrave has nothing to urge on Mr Wilson except that the British should soldier on. Like his predecessor in government, when he was in government, he has no policy on the North of Ireland.

It could be said that except for the brief and euphoric Sunningdale era, no Irish government since the treaty has had a policy on the North: as witness, amongst other things, the ease with which a text from Mr de Valera can be found to fit every change in Fianna Fáil attitudes.

Before Sunningdale, and before "the present troubles", stretching back to the dim origins of the Southern State, there was a sort of unity policy which was really no policy at all, more an assertion of the "unity principle" without any practical proposals to back it up, any threat of effective measures whether persuasive or punitive, or any sort of commitment to the winning of anybody's hearts and minds. And in so far as the assertion of the "unity principle" without any practical proposals to back it up constituted a policy, it was the worst one possible. It encouraged Northern Protestants to believe that Southern Irishmen, and Southern politicians in particular, were everything they in any case wanted to believe they were: weak, canting hypocrites, and at best thimble-riggers, more interested in fooling their own people than in getting anything done.

It also allowed Protestants to feel that they were being brave, defiant, steadfast, true to King and Country and prepared to fight to the death throughout a fifty year period in which nobody, not even the IRA, posed any sort of serious threat to whatever liberties or otherwise they were supposed to be enjoying. The siege mentality therefore had fifty years of existence and fifty years of careful nurturing before it was put to any sort of real test: fifty years in which it prevented the growth of class consciousness, concealed the real facts of life from the voters, and, pathetically where the majority of Protestants were concerned, sharpened the Protestant sense of difference and the Protestant sense of victorious superiority.

But the fact was that for all that Southern governments and even the Southern population in general actually intended, they could all have rested easy in the enjoyment of their privileges, real or imaginary. Apart from a vague and vaguely expressed wish for unity, before Sunningdale (which was a typical, British-inspired non-event) no Irish government has had a policy on the North of Ireland.

Let it be said for them, however, that they are not the only grouping of politicians, in or out of office, to have no policy on the North. At this moment, following the collapse of the second convention, none of the major groupings in the North itself have any policy whatever — or any realisable policy, which is much the same thing.

Let us take the minority's elected representatives first. One of the strange things about the early days of the present historical episode was the surprise everybody in Britain and Southern Ireland felt that the northern minority suffered so much. The sympathy felt for them was immense and extraordinary and, although it included an element of guilt, it included also an element of euphoria, that which is produced by being on the right side, the sort of thing liberals always feel when they sympathise with those who have been hard done by. But at the same time it was a bit unclear what they wanted most, unity or equality; and the fact that it was not clear, least of all to the minority themselves, allowed for enormous ambiguities of attitude on everybody's part, including that of their elected representatives.

The fact is that the SDLP draws, and has always drawn, many of its votes from "republicans" who allegedly want unity. It draws many others from those who want such things as housing and job equality. It has a wide spectrum of support which is simply concerned with its dignity as citizens, or, less worthily perhaps, with its status as members of a tribe. And it includes among its most active elements politicians who, whether they know it or not, primarily want politics.

At the beginning it must have seemed to many that the attainment of one objective — political equality — would necessarily and perhaps even probably bring about the other — national unity. There were those who wanted unity but spoke most often of equality because it seemed to suit the situation. There were those who primarily wanted unity but grew afraid to speak of it and spoke most often of equality because it seemed more realistic. There were those who simply wanted revenge, or at least some sort of squaring of accounts. And, naturally enough, those who were politically inclined wanted politics.

But politics includes office, or the possibility of a victory and a prize. It does not exist *in vacuo*. And whether its inclusion among the fundamental human rights could be justified or not, the denial of politics to those who are inclined that way (and they are many) is felt as more iksome than the denial of many other things, irrespective of what the politics are supposed to be "for".

Generally speaking the lower down you go on the social scale among Catholics the more "the republic" (that is unity) is wanted and the higher you go the more regard is set on other things, including politics. That is not to say that the people in the ghettos do not care about jobs and housing also; but is to assert that apart from those who have a real "republican" tradition, Catholics at the lower end of the social scale do, understandably, feel a continuing physical threat to their very existence which they believe unity, making them automatically members of the governing majority, would end.

As a way of reconciling all these desires and confusions, the practical with impractical alike in the midst of a situation which fluctuated day by day and in which it was desirable not to appear either too moderate or too extreme, "power-sharing" and the "Irish dimension" came as a god-send to the minority representatives. Even stripped of the "Irish dimension", "power sharing" remained a plausible objective. That it was a dead-end all along could be argued, for, apart from being an attempt at compromise all round, Sunningdale was even an attempt at compromise about the minority's objectives on the part of the representatives of the northern minority itself, and to some extent it was brought down by the intransigence of those within the minority for whom it was not enough. But that it is a dead-end now anyway must be obvious, for even if it were to be forced on the representatives of the majority by a referendum which they could conceivably lose, with whom would the SDLP share power? And is there really much future in membership of an imposed government in a drastically worsening economic situation when the real power to alter that situation — the money-power — remains, as it will remain, unused in Westminster?

But if the representatives of the minority are now without policy (and have been, in a concealed fashion, for some time) the representatives of the majority are similarly bereft. They too include among their supporters people who want differing things; law and order, in any case and by any means; law and order under the crown, with the maintenance of democratic forms and formulae; the restoration of the Protestant supremacy through the ballot box; the rule of the democratic majority (or is it the democratic rule of the majority?) Government according to the British model; Government from Westminster itself; but in any case, and whatever form of Government it may be, politics both as a mode in itself and as a possible means to office. And the fact is that in the present situation most of these things are unattainable, just as "power-sharing" for the other side has proved unattainable and "unity" or even the vaguest ghost or shadow of it even more so.

Some of them are not attainable because the only means to their own hand for either side are negative means, and although you can bring a regime down by bombs or riots or general strikes you cannot create one by them. Some of them are not attainable because the long-awaited defeat of the Provisional IRA has not happened, the British, who have the means, not having, according to the majority, the real will to do the job. And some of them are not attainable because they are in the British gift and under no conceivable cirumstances could the British grant them and remain responsible for the situation: whatever world opinion might or might not say the minority would prove utterly ungovernable if they came about and the British know this and therefore will not allow them to be brought about while they have the responsibility. Some, of course, are simply not attainable because they conflict, like "unity" and "power-sharing", with other objectives which the same politician allegedly has and on the maintenance of which he depends for a large body of his support.

But, it will be noted, in all the confused, self-contradictory and often unattainable objectives of both the majority and the minority one peculiar factor constantly recurs. Some of them are dependent on the British for their possible implementation or imposition; and others are at the same time rendered barren of fruition by the very same force. British power to both sides, and at the same time, means hope and "No Road". British power in fact, in the last analysis, means stasis and only stasis.

From the British point of view, their very presence on the spot and the fact that they have the apparent power to implement any policy means that totally unrealistic and often contradictory policy suggestions will continue to be made to them. From the politicians' point of view it means either that (as in the case of successive Southern governments) you need not make any proposals at all, self-contradictory, constructive or whatever; or else, like all the Northern parties, you can regard everything as an interim step and encourage within your own breast and the breasts of your supporters contradictory aspirations as well as mere means of magically continuing with politics without any final or dreadful political result.

But in any case it means stasis: and in fact it might seem at first glance as if there was only one thing the British could do which would really alter the situation and that would be to withdraw. Such an impression would not, however, be correct. There is one other course of action which the British might take: they could declare, today or tomorrow, their intention to withdraw, in five years' or ten. That such a declaration would have an effect on the situation nobody doubts. Where opinions, to say the least of it, differ, is about what sort of an effect it might be.

The Famous Declaration

WE ARE told we must not be for the "Declaration of Intent" because that is to play somebody's game, to encourage the men of violence to believe that the thing they have been waiting for is only round the corner. We are told further that the only hope of peace is that the British should remain; that a British withdrawal certainly and a declaration of intent almost inevitably would be followed by violence and bloodshed. Those who use this latter argument might seem to some of us to be saying, in the words of the prophet Jeremiah, "peace, peace, when there is no peace": for the truth is that the North Eastern corner of this island has been suffering terrible things under the aegis of the peace-keepers for five, going on six long years; that it is suffering at this moment much more than the South has any clear conception of; and that no practical proposals premising an indefinite British presence are any longer emerging from anywhere which are likely to bring this suffering to an end.

Nor, apart from the vague hope that the Faulknerite Unionists and the followers of Mr Craig will somehow win a majority of loyalist opinion to their side and will thereafter admit the representatives of the minority on sufferance to a Government which would last long enough to accomplish anything (supposing there is anything within the sphere of government which it could accomplish) is there even any sign of a drift or tendency towards peace in the present situation. It will be noted that those who speak of the British remaining do not make use of the little phrase "for ever" when they do so; and yet, even if they do remain for ever, from what quarter is peace to come?

Dr Conor Cruise O'Brien has recently been debating the issue with Mr John Robb. Mr Robb says that a British disengagement is inevitable and it is important that it should be a controlled disengagement. The longer we wait for this to happen the more sudden it may be and the more disastrous the consequences. Dr O'Brien replies that he has no reason to believe the British are contemplating any such thing and that he has confidence in their remaining as long as they have to; but then he adds that to mention the possibility of British withdrawal increases its probability. Mr

Robb winds up by declaring his belief in the desirability of such an announcement to withdraw because it is the only thing which could conceivably bring about any change in the situation: and he adds that in the situation as it exists the North is suffering too much.

And Mr Robb is of course right. The choice is really between a continuing British presence with a continuing waste and carnage of the sort which has grown so monstrously familiar: and a British declaration to withdraw which could have either evil consequences or good.

One says either/or because no man can be certain. We are all in the words of Thomas Jefferson, "advancing rapidly to destinies beyond the reach of mortal eye"; and nobody has a right to pretend that he is sure of anything in the present situation, though most of the men of power feel compelled to keep up an appearance of certainty about everything. There is a school of thought which believes that the British presence in this island must in any case and in the face of any consequence be brought to an end; and with that point of view, lest there should be any question of concealed interests, the present writer had better say that he has a great deal of sympathy. He believes that a certain reading of history will show that Wolfe Tone was more or less right. Britain has been the never failing source of most of our evils, even down to the cynical failure to make any attempt to work the Act of Union – which might, which just might, have been Ireland's salvation – until its authors were frightened by a recrudescence of Irish nationalism 80 years after it was passed: while Britain has equally certainly in modern times and ancient been the source of most of the woes and the reason for the false position occupied by the erstwhile planter (or, more accurately, transplanted) population of the North.

But that is not the ground on which the present argument proceeds. The present argument is between those whose desperate hope, insofar as they have any hope, is in the indefinite continuance of the present awful state of affairs, and those who believe that the consequences of a British declaration of intent would be more likely to be good than bad; and that the risk to the contrary is therefore a risk that ought to be taken. To the first point of view the government pins its faith, such as it is; and to that point of view Mr Lynch, while he was in office, pinned his faith also.

Of course the real moment for the declaration of intent was four or five or even six years ago before the rise of the Protestant private armies and the large-scale gun-running that made them possible. If at that time the South had spoken with any confidence as to its ability, its courage and its will, it is possible that by now a settlement would have been arrived at and even that that settlement would have been a form of unity, for the Southern government was, after all, the natural authority in this island, fulfilling the requirements which Imperial powers are accustomed to look for when eventually they depart. It was at that time the only authority which could have guaranteed the safety of both Protestants and Catholics; for the Catholics, to be brief about it, would not have been in any danger of attack, while the Southern government would have been able to restrain them from attacking anyone else, supposing they had the wish to do so. Withdrawing in the proper way and with a properly contrived handover, the Imperial power would also have been able to ensure that there was neither anarchy nor revolution in the province which it left and that its basic economic structure and connections would remain intact — these being the arrangements closest to the hearts of Imperial powers when they repent of their imperium.

The right course of action for a Southern government at that time would have been to urge on the British that they should remain only so long as it took to transfer power to another authority (preferably themselves) in an orderly fashion; but even at a somewhat later stage the thing to insist on would have been that which would have put an end to the vague and contradictory hopes Loyalist politicians have been so adept at encouraging in their supporters: in other words a declaration that the British connection would within a stated period of time come to an end and that whatever provisions were to be made for the economic well-being of the North-eastern corner of this island (or the island as a whole) would be subject to stern negotiation in the interval.

In the fullness of time, however, the declaration of intent to withdraw had been established in everybody's minds as the policy of the Provisional IRA and Kevin Street Sinn Féin. The damnable law by which politicians cannot yield the credit for having had the proper policy objective (we are not talking about policy means) to any other grouping, let alone to men of violence, had begun to be a governing factor. Then came Sunningdale and the curious baseless euphoria which as a consequence began to possess the politicians and to pervade the media and the editorials written in the Southern portion of this island. Sunningdale was the ideal solution. The British were withdrawing anyway. The Irish dimension would inevitably extend itself. Because the men of real power in the North (the Protestant business community) were hard-headed realists who would hasten to ingratiate themselves with the new order, not only reconciliation but unity itself was just around the corner.

Well, as we all know now, it was poppycock; and when a new power emerged among the Protestant workers (to whatever extent still the victims of political manipulation) and Sunningdale collapsed our Government was rendered, as it still remains, policyless; while the "Declaration of Intent" still remains Provisional policy and is for that reason, as well as others, still untouchable.

The principal one among the others is the well-known adage that the devil we know is better than the devil we don't. The fact that the devil we know stalks the streets and haunts the roadways of the North nightly does not matter. The greater devil that our fears conjure up would be worse. We have been brainwashed, or brainwashed ourselves, into a desparate trust in the British presence and frightened even out of any discussion of the matter on the grounds that mere discussion of any alternative whatever may weaken the conviction in higher British circles that that presence is essential.

Besides "playing into the hands of 'the men of violence' " and encouraging them to continue for even a day longer, raising the possibility of a British withdrawal would signal a new period of struggle on all sides which would eventually result in a bloody civil war. The appeal is at once to our humanity, our fears and to the sort of organic optimism that always grows in the human mind during the mere continuance of any situation however dreadful. It is constantly said, for example, that a hope resides in the mere perpetuation of politics, or, when politics collapse, in the revival of politics under British guidance, but the fact is that when politics revives bloodshed increases; and it is in the present situation of alternative politics and no politics that the threat of civil war has grown and receives encouragement — for there are those among the politicans whose business it is to encourage and manipulate it and use it even to bring politics back (with the hope of power) when all other hope in politics has gone.

And then there is the suggestion that we in the South have no right to speak of or to discuss these things at all. The answer to this is that we too are compelled to watch, if not to suffer, the constant degradation of human nature and the image of Ireland; that we too live under the threat of bad becoming worse until eventually civil war itself is the outcome; and finally like it or not like it, and whatever definitions of a "country" are involved, this is our country too.

Still, the pressures are immense; the temptation to do nothing and to say nothing is strong, and it is indeed a brave man who risks even the psychological trauma involved, let alone the forms of obloquy which will possibly be incurred. For these reasons Mr Lynch, who has restored the "Declaration of Intent" to a wider area of political debate, is to be congratulated on an act of statesmanship.

Such acts do not often or always pay off in votes and that this particular one did not was plain for all to see in Mayo West. We would be in a sad case though if all political policy were dictated by the expediency of the moment. Mr Lynch has provided an alternative; and whatever Fianna Fáil's shortcomings in the past they are now performing the duty of an opposition, more especially since their support for such a declaration was couched in reasonable terms and took an adequately long view.

For no-one in the end, not even, as I understand them, the men of violence, is talking about a British withdrawal in one year or two. Five years have been mentioned and even fifteen, which, incidentally, was the period set for the reconsideration of the future of the Saar Basin after the First World War. Eight or ten years is probably a realistic period for the British to declare, but when they do declare it they must be firm and unambiguous about it. There should be no extensions and no reconsiderations of the basics which they may eventually lay down, though to begin with at least any suggestion coming from any quarter, elected or otherwise, about the future of the six counties or their individual or collective relationship either with the rest of Ireland or with any place else should be considered. Probably the best way to consider them is by way of a Commission in relation to which the elected politicians might be given some sort of role; and the period set could be divided into two halves; one for consideration and discussion and one for firm preparation and implementation; say four or five years for each.

One result such a Declaration might have straight away. If the Provisionals choose they can be statesmanlike and accept it as a fulfilment of the demand they have been making all along. They should then suspend aggressive action and leave the blame for whatever might occur on those whom it would then become the plain duty of the British government to contain and, eventually, to disarm. Unlike a vulnerable political regime with no real existence except by the consent of various factions in the North itself, the Westminster government, in implementing the consequences of a declaration for the long-term future would not be at the mercy of such action as was taken during the loyalist strike; and if the declaration were made with sufficient clarity and firmness it ought to be apparent that such action would be useless anyway. Besides which, can anybody really believe that the will to further conflict and the thirst for blood would survive such an eight or ten year period, more particularly since the more intransigent would be losing ground all the time to those who had some conception of a settlement in which they were willing to co-operate?

But even the threat of civil war occurring at the end of an eight or ten year period might shock certain people into the realisation that it is necessary to be reasonable and imaginative and constructive and co-operative and all the other things that they are not being at the moment. If they were these things, who knows what wonders might not emerge? Certain it is at least that nothing shows any signs of emerging from the present situation, nor is it even clear any longer for what we are supposed to be waiting and hoping.

> Then, said I, Lord, how long? And he answered: Until the cities be wasted without inhabitants and the houses without man, and the land be utterly desolate, and the Lord have removed men far away and there be a great forsaking in the midst of the land.

Is that what we are supposed to be waiting for?

H-Block

THE HISTORY of British rule in Ireland has been marked by the gravest miscalculations of public opinion, the most ironic reversals of intended effect and the most surprising recrudescences of fortune on the part of Britain's apparently defeated enemies. It has also, unfortunately for the relations between the two countries, been marked by hypocrisies and duplicities far beyond the normal run of British policy elsewhere.

It is now beginning to seem likely that in spite of the much-heralded enlightenments of British policy over the last ten years or so we are witnessing one of those situations in which hypocrisy and miscalculation combine to produce an effect grotesquely other than that originally or ostensibly intended.

The increasingly grim and sordid H-Block situation is now just over two years old: to be precise the first prisoner involved, Kieran Nugent, has been refusing to wear prison clothes or to do prison work since September 14th, 1976. At that time (in the summer of 1976) the concerted attempt, north and south, to "criminalise" the IRA appeared likely to have a fair chance of success. Commonly referred to as thugs, gangsters, bullies and hoodlums, the Provisionals had lost (forfeited if you like) so much sympathy even among erstwhile supporters that the process of branding them as ordinary lawbreakers seemed to need little formal ratification. When the Secretary of State for Northern Ireland decided that no prisoner convicted for a crime committed after March 1976 should be accorded exceptional or political status in the prisons of the Six Counties, he must have thought that in whatever resulted, he would have the backing of very large numbers of people, even in the Catholic areas.

What did result at the time was a refusal on the part of Provisional prisoners to accept "ordinary convict" status: they would neither wear the regulation garb nor perform the regulation tasks. In an attempt to smash their resistance as quickly as possible, the authorities imposed punishments which amounted to locking them in their cells for the full twenty-four hours each day without reading material or any other form of distraction, entertainment or information. The prisoners reacted by refusing to wash and slop out; and they thus began a situation in which an increasing number of naked men are living in conditions of mental and physical deprivation involving filth and misery so extreme that they are difficult as well as unpleasant to imagine.

At present the authorities have resorted to forcible bathing and scrubbing of reluctant prisoners and hosing down the cells, leaving the naked prisoners to lie afterwards on wet mattresses. Jaundice, ringworm, dermatitis and un-named rashes are now said to be common, but partly because any report of an ailment is followed by the forcible bathing and scrubbing which they allege involves ill-treatment, the prisoners are reluctant to report them and worse diseases on an epidemic scale are likely to result any day.

Now, although in part all this has come about because of the prisoners' refusal to co-operate, it has its origins in the refusal on the part of the Crown to treat them as being exceptional in any way. They are, say the authorities, part of the common run of convicted criminals and ought to be treated as such. But by one of the grim paradoxes attendant on the whole situation, what this refusal has done is to call attention to the fact that the men in H-Block are in every way exceptional: not only in their fortitude, their discipline and their resolve, but equally important from the Secretary of State's point of view, in the circumstances surrounding their conviction.

More people than ever before are now aware that about many of these convictions there are serious doubts, both in law and in fact. Eighty per cent of those in H-Block were charged on the evidence of statements extracted from them in circumstances which, everyone must admit, leave a lot to be desired; 76.6% of them were found guilty on the evidence of such statements alone. Even if one were to believe that the overwhelming probability is that these men are or were members of a particular organisation, and even if one belonged to the number of people who say that no mercy should be accorded to those who are members of that organisation, we are a long way from the "ordinary convicted criminal" line of argument.

The law by which these men were convicted is an emergency law: in the British system of justice, exceptional. The courts in which they are convicted are emergency courts: again in the British system of justice, exceptional. The sentences which they are serving are in many cases — contrary perhaps to popular belief — of exceptional severity in relation to the specific crime involved. Everything about them is exceptional except the conditions of servitude which the authorities are prepared to go to such lengths to impose on them. In the words of Fathers Faul and Murray:

> These men were sentenced by *special* courts after being interrogated by *special* methods under detention by emergency *special* laws and sentenced to *special* long sentences; yet any claim they may make to have a *special* category status in the prison is denied.

In fact, inherent in the policy of "criminalisation" and essential to the long-term objectives of its devisers was the assertion that Northern Ireland was itself basically a normal society, or a society in the process of returning to normality. It had admittedly been rent by differences, but these were not so insuperable as not to be amenable to solution by the processes of democracy and law. And unfortunately from the point of view of those in authority, the H-Block situation does nothing but underline once again the fact that things in reality are altogether otherwise.

Northern Ireland is a society in which nearly three thousand people are imprisoned who could not be tried by the ordinary processes of law and who cannot be punished by them either. Without this particular piece of double-think on the Secretary of State's part, the shaky foundation on which the law still rests in Northern Ireland would not be so appallingly obvious.

Worse still, perhaps, from his point of view is the underlining of the fact that the men concerned are everything but criminals in the ordinary − or any − sense of the word. Ordinary criminals − if such exist − have, to put it mildly, far more sense than to undergo voluntarily the forms of physical and mental deprivation and degradation that the men of H-Block are prepared to endure. It may be alleged in some quarters that they endure them only because they are subject to a ruthless discipline. Whether or not that is true (and in the view of the present writer, it is far from the truth) the fact remains that they endure them; that they seem prepared to go on enduring them; and that in this horrible contest of wills it is, so far, the Secretary of State's Office which has come off worst.

And therein lies the final failure of the process of criminalisation. Increasingly, since the nature of the H-Block situation was borne in on the general consciousness, the use of simplistic words such as hoodlum and gangster has become less common; the allegation that Provisional and other activity was all some kind of gigantic extortion racket has been heard less often. Ordinary bank robbers and the operators of protection rackets in general are not the stuff of which H-Block prisoners are made.

And, intolerable though the present situation is, in the exposure of this particular untruth may lie the seeds of some kind of development in the future. No matter what one's aims and objects in any situation, it is essential to know the nature of the people with whom you deal; but in the employment of a certain kind of terminology about the membership of the Provisional IRA and other organisations − in the ultimate belief even that this terminology was accurate − governments and leaders of public opinion, North and South, unfitted themselves in a very serious way to comprehend or to deal with or to find any way out of the historical situation in which we find ourselves.

There are at present roughly two thousand "Catholic or Republican" political prisoners in the north-eastern part of Ireland. They all, at the very least, have relatives and friends and beyond these relatives and friends there are numerous supporters and well-wishers who know them, or to whom they are known. To suppose that these people are all well-wishers and supporters of a corrupt and merely criminal conspiracy is to unfit yourself to deal with the situation as it stands. Worse still, perhaps, it is to let yourself in for the most appalling kind of surprises in the future.

October 1978

Pomp and Circumstance

AS I write the funeral of Lord Mountbatten is being televised. It is elaborate, solemn, beautifully managed and, on a certain level, moving. The service recruits, besides the sober liturgy of the Church of England and the talents of churchmen of other persuasions, two marvellous poems (one more marvellous than the other, but both marvellous nonetheless): Kipling's "Recessional" and William Blake's "Jerusalem".

> Far-called, our navies melt away
> On dune and headland sinks the fire
> Lo all our pomp of yesterday
> Is one with Nineveh and Tyre.

And

> I shall not cease from mental strife
> Nor shall my sword sleep in my hand
> Till we have built Jerusalem
> In England's green and pleasant land.

As I watch I feel that it would require only a little Keatsian suspension of belief, attitude or point of view, a little loss of identity, to enter totally into the spirit of this elaborate and elegiac pageantry, to feel lifted and annealed by the strains of the slow march, the Gothic harmonies of Westminster Cathedral, the solemn saluting, the clear and lingering notes of the last post.

Since, like most of those who deal in words or imaginative conceptions, like most of the poetic tribe, I am, as Keats pointed out, subject to such losses of identity, it would certainly not be difficult: it would be a negative, rather than a positive thing, a mere yielding to the weight of centuries of tradition, the respect for bravery and martial skill which is bred in all of us, the respect, even, for civilisation and civic harmony as represented by England's almost miraculous continuity of tradition. And there would be besides the knowledge that the forces of barbarism are not always easily kept at bay; that the war in which Mountbatten so distinguished himself was fought against such forces; that there is a sense (even an intellectual sense) in which Westminster Abbey and what is gathered therein partly symbolises what stands between us and the recrudescence of such forces in our world.

Since, however, I do not allow myself such a Keatsian — Keats would have said Shakespearean — suspension, I remain somewhat outside it all. I do not join in this apparent consensus. The harmonies, the catharsis that others and — if we are to judge from Brian Farrell's commentary — large numbers of people in this country are experiencing are, in a sense, denied me. In part what shuts me out from them — or them from me — is a set of beliefs about the divisions of interest in English — in any — society and how these divisions are masked and concealed by ceremonial occasions of grief or rejoicing, by the banner, by the flag, by the crown, in part a reflection on what should be the aims and purposes of civilisation itself and how they are disguised and even caricatured by the sort of pomp and pageantry we are witnessing.

But there is also something more. England is a country which, superficially at least, has attained to that unbroken plateau of civilisation to which all communities aspire. There, superficially at least, those who truly represent the national interest do no wrong. They act in accordance with the rule of law, out of patriotic motives and with no reference to their broad acres or their business interests. To be Irish, on the contrary, is to be aware of fierce complexities, contradictions and divisions: to be constantly, one might even say, in the wrong. Otherwise it is to accept a cliché less justified by the nature of Irish life than is the English cliché: a cliché born of mere panic, emulation, or desire to be rid of these complexities: or perhaps born only of naked self-interest. I prefer to be Irish. I prefer not to accept the cliché.

What I am trying to say has difficulties and pitfalls of an even more-than-usual order, and so the reader must bear with me. The fortunate ones in any situation are those who feel only one emotion, one grief at a time. Blessed are those who find life simple. But in trying to say it (whatever it is) let me call to my aid two texts: one from a figure known and respected for his sincercity and regard for truth by thousands; the other from a correspondent whose name is unknown to me at least, but whose sincerity is evident in what he writes. Let me take him first.

Mr P. N. Synnott says that; "Lord Mountbatten had never deliberately done any harm to any other person." It is the sort of statement that one passes over without question — perhaps one should, in another sense, pass over it now. But the fact remains that Louis Mountbatten's profession was war. After being chief of Combined Operations — a sphere of activity in which dirty killing was practically the name of the game — he became Supreme

Commander in an area where the world conflict was being fought out with particular ferocity. The campaign against Japan, in which he must have been privy to the highest decisions, culminated in the dropping of the atom bombs on Hiroshima and Nagasaki. The very funeral which I have just been watching was in large part a celebration of his eminence, skill, courage and ruthlessness in the killing of other human beings.

From the gun carriage on which his body lay to the six Fox Armoured Reconaissance Vehicles which escorted it from the Abbey it was full of reminders that war is a serious, not just a ceremonial business. Admittedly, Mountbatten's killing was "patriotic". Admittedly the wars in which he participated were "declared" wars for which the English people's consent had been obtained by one means of persuasion or another; and the second conflict was one in which, for once, there was almost in moral terms, a black and a white. Admittedly the English have a genius for being in the right. Further than these things, he was a man of some humanity and moderately progressive views (I myself was in Tory company one evening in 1952 when he was described as a "red" and accused of being practically a Soviet agent by Auberon Herbert).

But the fact remains that neither in terms of his profession or (some would say) his place in the scheme of things could it be said of him that he had "never deliberately done any harm to any other person". He did appalling harm to hundreds of thousands, perhaps even millions. That he meant to do it, that he did it for the best and most patriotic reasons, that he comported himself with dignity while he did it — all this is true, but the fact remains that he did it; and did it cheerfully and with some panache.

Now nothing that is said here is to be interpreted as being equivalent to saying that because he himself was a retired naval officer who had done some pretty things in his time, the Provisional IRA were justified in killing him. And of course it would not be worth labouring this point about an old man suddenly and brutally taken at the end of his days, or taking Mr Synnott's innocent enough phrase and holding it up to the light in this particular way, if there weren't something larger involved. But there is. There is the flight from the harsh complexities of our situation into unthinking clichés: from an attempt to rethink the whole dreary business into the cosier forms of self-abnegation and self-abasement. The one robs us of all insight; the other of all powers of decision.

Lord Mountbatten was killed by men of violence who in terms of the cause that they serve have decided to be cold-blooded and indifferent to the individual's right to live. True we are not talking about the jungles of south-east Asia but about a peaceful Sligo village, but there is nothing whatever to be gained from beating our breasts and declaring that this cold-bloodedness or this indifference are specifically and horribly Irish characteristics. They are not.

Which brings me to the second text — one I approach with great diffidence because the author of it is Bishop Cathal Daly and because, by accident, I do not have his exact words by me. However, to the best of my recollection what the Bishop said (or was quoted as saying) recently was that these appalling deeds were of such a nature that one was driven to the conclusion that the ideology behind them must be something from outside, something utterly alien to Ireland and the Irish people. This may, perhaps, be an expression of the belief that the Provisional IRA is a Marxist-inspired or dominated organisation. If so, they are based on an untruth. The Provisional IRA may have strands in its motivations, but in so far as we can speak of ideologies and not attitudes, I would beg the Bishop to enquire truly in his heart of hearts whether, as others say with different motives than mine, its ideologies are not native born, native reared and native nurtured. So native are they, in my belief, that there is scarcely any second-generation inheritor in this state who does not owe something to that ideological stance, or that fundamental attitude: there is scarcely anybody who is or has been in office and in power who does not.

The Catholic Church owes a great deal to it and its persistence over the years; and the Protestant Church to its mere circumstantial (not moral) obverse. Bishop Daly knows, I should judge, as well as I do that the hand-washings which come out of this sort of consciousness are not always as admirable as they sound. Since his belief is rebirth, he must know that rebirths are (and should be) difficult and painful things and are not to be achieved either by repetition of any cliché or by shocked disownment of the things that have made the world you live in.

What is to the point is that when Mr Lynch went to London this week, he should have had a policy. Indeed he has one, if he could but have enunciated it or returned to it. That, as I write, he seems unlikely to do either is as much due to the flight into the cliché as it is to anything else. Every time something like this happens, we retreat into shock and self-abasement and fail to face the difficulties of urging on others the only way forward that either country can take.

September 1979

Till the Boys Come Home

THE 60th anniversary of the bloody battle of the Somme has been responsible for a lot of discussion of war and its causes in general and of the Great War and its causes in particular. Considering the appalling nature of that conflict and its still untold and unnumbered consequences for civilisation and human psychology, this is no wonder. But a good deal of the discussion only goes to show in what cursory fashion everybody, including historians, examines history and how little grasp everybody, including historians, has of human motive.

Thus among the more fatuous of the alleged truisms trotted out again was that the Great War was caused by "rival nationalisms" and that the sort of young men who were members of Kitchener's army and went up to the Somme in the last days of June, 1916, were motivated by "nationalistic fervour".

The powers that rushed into conflict with each other in August, 1914, were imperial powers and they had, one and all, imperial interests. As David Thomson has shown, the war at its beginning was one between great powers and great powers only.

> Of the smaller States, only Serbia and Belgium were implicated, in both cases because they were attacked by great powers. Italy kept out for nearly a year, and Portugal had to be discouraged by Britain from entering the war on her side.

This is true, but we could, of course, go further and point out that the analogy so often drawn by local orators outside Church doors in 1914 and 1915 — drawn indeed on that fateful Sunday and in that fatal impromptu speech at Woodenbridge — between "gallant little Belgium" and its aspirations to be left in peace, and independence and Ireland and its hopes for ditto, was absolute balderdash. Even Belgium, apart from Serbia the smallest of the original countries involved, was master of almost a million square miles and upwards of twenty million people in central Africa. Alone among those involved, Serbia was a merely national entity; and while its boundaries did not even include all the Serbs, never mind the Croats and Slovenes, Serbia was nevertheless attacked. It is true that it was a member of the Serbian "Black Hand" secret society who precipitated the whole business by assassinating the Archduke Ferdinand; but, as Liddell Hart has pointed out:

> ... his death was most welcome to Austrian officialdom. It gave them the opportunity of executing their own designs under the excuse of avenging the man whose accession to the throne they had feared. By crushing Serbia they hoped to cement the Austrian empire against the Slav movement within its borders, while establishing its ascendancy in the Balkans.

The point is that nationalism, in any proper meaning of the word, is always a defensive force. Even the killing of the Archduke was a defensive act, a counter-measure against the annexation in 1908 of Bosnia and Herzegovina; but if indeed the aim of the killing had in fact been the loosening of Austria's hold on her Serbian population, then that would have been, in any terms that allow of the right of nations to exist at all, defensive too, just as the Irish rebellion of Easter 1916 was, in those terms, defensive.

But if nationalism is, in any reasonable, proper meaning of the word, a defensive force, imperialism is, in any meaning at all, an aggressive one; and the powers that went to war were, as has been said, imperialist powers. Even if not always in the Leninist sense (the movement of finance capital looking for outlets and of industry looking for markets) imperialism is always aggressive and always leads to war. The fact is that the existence of an imperial power is an act of aggression in itself; and that militarism is its necessary coefficient and ideological appurtenance.

On the relationship of the individual psychology of people in high places to the forces they control, or which control them and may eventually destroy them, two quotations. The first, from Liddell Hart on the psychology of Austrian officialdom, follows directly after the last sentence quoted from him above:

> And in consolidating the empire each member of the ruling body had the hope of consolidating his own position.

The second, from Thucydidates, concerns the psychology of the war-makers at the top throughout the ages, and the passage of time has not dimmed or weakened its melancholy force:

> That war is an evil is something that we all know, and it would be pointless to go on cataloguing all the disadvantages involved in it. No one is forced into war by ignorance, nor, if he thinks he will gain from it, is he kept out of it by fear. The fact is that one side thinks that the profits to be won outweigh the risks to be incurred, and the other side is ready to face danger rather than accept an immediate loss.

The psychology of those who rushed to do the fighting is, of course, another matter; but to attribute it primarily to nationalism is ludicrous in the extreme. Millions of people in all the combatant countries may have been codded into thinking that the customs and moral conventions, the familiar sights and reassurances of the home and heart-land were somehow in danger from the dark-intentioned enemy without, but that is as far as nationalism went. Where the sort of young clerks and cricket lovers, factory-workers and pigeon fanciers who went up to the Somme were concerned, even that would have been thin enough wine. What sent them to their deaths were the degraded vestiges of European romantic chivalry, the glorification of honour and gallantry which were in everything they heard or read in that old world. Public-schoolboy and cotton-operative were alike victims of an ancient code, involving the plighting of one's life, the proof of bravery and the guerdon that awaited all who survived the test. John Redmond, doubtless no less a victim than anyone else, spoke at Woodenbridge, be it remarked, not only of the war being "undertaken in defence of the highest principles of religion and morality and right," but, almost incredibly now, of "the duty of proving on the field of battle that gallantry and courage which has distinguished our race all through its history."

There were those who went for pay and there were those who went for bread; but the spirit of the Somme was the spirit of adventure; and the origins of that dreadful battle are to be found in the horrible ideals of the Catholic Middle Ages and in the horrible idealisation and separation of men and women which chivalrous romance implied. And if we ask how this strange thing cropped up again in the urbanised and industrialised world of the late Victorian and Edwardian era, and why it flowered so rapidly in the novels and poetry of the age as to mislead and destroy a generation, we must I think also ask how imperialist aggression of any kind could have sustained itself for long without this very exaltation of adventure. The darker forces of the age called on the false poetic morality of a long dead era to glorify its work for it, and we all know now how it answered.

The Brotherhood of Man

THE HALF-HEARTED General Strike which took place in Britain fifty years ago this week had one curious and not very often remarked-on consequence. In Russia in the previous year, Stalin had prevailed on the fourteenth Party Congress to adopt the doctrine of "Socialism in one country." The thesis was that the spate of post-war revolution in Europe had fizzled out; that world upheaval must be abandoned as any sort of practical ideal; and that the Russians had better concentrate on going it alone.

But the argument was by no means over. In January 1925 Trotsky had been relieved of his post as commissar for war, but he was still a member both of the politbureau and of the party. And now, to raise the hopes of those who alleged, as he did, that revolution in one or other of the advanced countries of Europe was still a possibility and might accompany and ensure the achievement of socialism in Russia came, of all things, the British General Strike.

The hopes, such as they were, did not last long. The "olive branches" referred to in Ramsay Mcdonald's rambling speech to the House of Commons on the night the strike began were all too assiduously held forth by the General Council of the Trades Union Congress throughout the subsequent proceedings; and the same orator's "angels of peace" proved to have a less ethereal and perhaps somewhat more sinister existence than the angels of Mons. From the Trotskyist point of view, as well as from the more immediate one of the soon-to-be abandoned coal miners, the British General Strike was a wash-out. The following year Trotsky was expelled from the party and exiled to Alma-Ata. "Socialism in one country" became the rigorously proclaimed and ensured policy of the Soviet Union.

Looked at in one way, there is little doubt that the policy was a success. If the Russians had gone on actively encouraging revolution elsewhere; had not manipulated Comintern policy in the often mysterious way they did; and had not entered into the trading relations and forms of co-existence with the outside world which the doctrine entailed, they might well have been urgently and efficiently put out of business. Although that would have meant the end of Stalin, it would have meant the end of a functioning Soviet State as well. The horrors of Stalinism we now know all about. The horrors of a restored Something-Or-Other may well be worth a moment's imagining.

Socialism in one country meant also, however, that from that point on the interests of all other Communist parties and of all possible revolutions were subordinated to Russian designs and interests in no uncertain fashion. In 1929 the pretence that the Comintern had any existence or independence other than that conferred on it by Stalin was largely given up. Old-guard revolutionaries were summoned to Moscow to meet a mostly very dubious fate. Communist movements everywhere were cynically betrayed and abandoned whenever it suited (or, worse still, appeared to suit) Soviet foreign policy to abandon them; and the seventh and last prewar Comintern Congress was convened in 1935 only so that Russian policy, already decided, might be cursorily explained and rubber-stamped. For the most part, Communists elsewhere were stooges and they knew it.

The paradoxical result was that the defeat of the internationalist Trotsky resulted in an extraordinary internationalism of Communist policy. It might be really a Russianisation, but it was nothing if not uniform; and if good, old-fashioned patriotism was soon to be called back into existence in Russia, as far as Communists were concerned it was at a discount everywhere else — at least until the Resistance movements called it forth again for a while. Trotsky had said that "socialism in one country" and all that flowed from it meant the rebirth of the nation-state and the end of the brotherhood of man; but from the moment the doctrine was proclaimed national differences and modes of national response vanished from the Communist world as completely as if the brotherhood of man was already an accomplished fact. To that rather grotesque extent, Trotsky was wrong. He remained wrong until the twenty-fifth party congress recently sat and listened to the fraternal delegates in Moscow.

At this point in the history lesson, however, I would like to call the attention of my faithful readers to a quite extraordinary article by Mr Peregrene Worsthorne, which referred *inter alia* to the British General Strike and which appeared in last Sunday's *Telegraph*. Now Mr Worsthorne, in case my readers do not know, is the bluest of the blue. I do not mean in terms of his personal ancestry, for of that I am ignorant. He may, for all I know, be descended from good Yorkshire mining stock; but in his opinions anyway he is as blue as your boot, the highest High Tory it is possible to imagine; and it is this which makes the nature of his complaint all the more extraordinary.

Under the heading "Fatal Flaw in British Socialism" Mr Worsthorne put forward his conviction that "The essence of socialism is a very strong sense of community, since only if individuals are enormously concerned about the public good, about the general well-being, will they be prepared to subordinate their private or sectional interests to the interests of the nation as a whole."

"Fraternity is an essential part of successful socialism," he declared "but fraternity implies blood brotherhood, links and affinities of a fundamental kind which go beyond mere mutal convenience; links and affinities of race, history, language and common symbols." All of these he believed had been so "diluted in recent years as to be practically non-existent." Although the British were now being asked to glory in the General Strike or celebrate May Day as a national holiday, "rather as earlier generations stirred to the memory of Agincourt or Waterloo," it wouldn't do. Such an attitude to the past was too class-orientated. Socialism would therefore be a flop, and its authors would be increasingly compelled to fall back on compulsion to make it work.

Now, leaving aside the blood-brotherhood bit, which may be a little too strong for your taste or mine, Mr Worsthorne is probably in general right. Socialism, let alone communism, probably does require more of a sense of immediate community to make it work than the apostles of mere human brotherhood like to believe. If there are ingredients in a nation's history, or even in its historical myth, which sustain such a feeling of community, it is probably no sort of a preparation for socialism to abandon them as mere atavisms or condemn them as vestigial remains of a nationalism that belongs to the past. The sense of human brotherhood may be all very well as an ultimate aim, but unfortunately in the short term it is probably too thin a gruel.

Of course I speak in this instance in terms of our own poor country. Dear old England may be in an unfortunate position, in the sense that everything that was previously glorified was a symbol or a reflection either of class dominance or of imperial greed, to say nothing of trappings and accoutrements that were actually instruments of both. But Ireland is a different case. Not too long ago there was here a widespread belief that the past was a history of communally shared suffering; and not too long before that such a belief even included the majority of the planter population of the North. But now that "myth" is in the process of demolition. We may wonder both whether the demolition process is not a poor preparation for any sort of socialism; and whether indeed the historians and para-historians concerned are not obscurely serving another purpose of which they may be quite unconscious. For there was something else that the estimable Mr Worsthorne said which bears reflecting upon.

Towards the end of his article in fact he cheered up. If any sort of a socialist system was unlikely to work in England because of the general decline in patriotism, there was another system that would. What matter if "Parliament, local authorities, the Church of England, police, judiciary, the armed forces, trade unions, the city of London" were all "seen to have feet of clay?" Never mind that "the authority of the State, respect for its institutions and unifying myths of nationhood are never likely to be restored." Capitalism could still get on with the job. It did not need any stuff-and-nonsense about shared institutions or common purposes to thrive. "For a capitalist system this does not matter. A capitalist system can survive and prosper in such circumstances," as indeed the splendid economic recovery of the United States, achieved in the face of "a condition of national vacuum," sufficiently proved — not to mention postwar Germany, where "the public spirit had been debauched by evil uses, and the nation divided by conquest."

So there you have it. Capitalism has long known that all men are the same in their greeds and fears and that national feelings were only there to be exploited; and where they are not strong enough to be exploited any longer we may expect them now to be abandoned. The brotherhood of man as governed by the profit motive, and believing only in the "relative morality" which the profit motive bred, will be enshrined in every capitalist heart if not openly inscribed on every capitalist banner.

But what of socialists? Well, it is at least worth pointing out that the "internationalist" communist parties — that is, the ones totally orientated towards Moscow — have never, save on the Russian doorstep and within the old Slavophile fold, succeeded in bringing about a transformation of any kind, whether we call the result socialism or not. Only in Eastern Europe and within the old Russian sphere of influence have they ever even come to power. The brotherhood of man may be the only possible ultimate, but it isn't much of a driving force. And where the excesses of the larger State and the rule of its bureaucracy are concerned, it isn't much of a safeguard. In fact, as even the internal history of the Soviet Union amply proves, the brotherhood of man usually turns out to be the dominance of somebody else.

May 1976

Liberation All Round

THERE IS no male person on this earth who has not got a stake, and a considerable stake, in the emancipation of women. It is, after all, better to be the son of a free woman than of a bond slave or a servant; it is better to be the lover of a free woman than of a bond slave or a servant. And so on through all the possible relationships between men and women, including that most important, but in Ireland strangely neglected and discouraged one, friendship.

But the assumption that the men are already free and that all the women have to do is batter their way into an area of freedom and fulfilment which the men are already enjoying is, with all due respects to the angrier among the women, ridiculous. Not only does it ignore the gross differences in male freedom which depend on class or, which is roughly, but not quite the same thing, the possession of money, but it also ignores the tyrannies to which men in our society are specially subject: the forms of responsibility which ought to be, but are not, shared; the aggressive, thrustful, competitive image which men must live up to because men and women together have conspired to create it.

It is true that in all male dominated societies there are forms of advantage and areas of pleasure and fulfilment open to men which are denied to women. The simplest and most obvious example from the world of yesterday was the Dublin pub. Although hardly anybody in their sane and sober senses would invent the Dublin pub, or regard it as a suitable, let alone an ideal, place for discourse or sociability, such as it was the men had it to themselves. And they also had certain games and pastimes from which women were debarred or excluded, though as much by other women and by custom which women had played a part in creating as by men.

And there were and are further in all male dominated societies forms of specific exploitation and domination of women by men which are only rarely or accidently parallelled the other way round. In part the physical differences between the sexes account for these — the female prostitute is, for several reasons, a more practical proposition than the male — more often they owe their existence to the fact that women are not trained for or admitted to any but the less well-paid and most boring forms of employment.

But to claim that marriage is an institution which confers all the advantages on the male in our society is ludicrous. It is true that the Republic's failure to secularise its laws in accordance with elementary republican principle means that many women are still condemned to child-bearing by circumstance rather than by choice, and that this is frequently a matter of male ignorance and domination. Yet the average male is exploited in the marriage relationship at least as much as the average female, and he often gets as little out of it. He works as hard, or harder. He is prey to at least as many anxieties as the female is, and they are often much more realistic as well as more acute.

If the relationship is neither harmonious nor fulfilling it is often as much her fault as his. To claim otherwise, at least where the sexual part of the relationship is concerned, is to admit that the woman's role is a passive one — an admission which many women are, quite properly, refusing to make. If male violence in the marriage situation is better publicised and attracts more attention from the law than female violence, that is only because female violence is, for anatomical reasons, more often verbal, but nonetheless destructive or injurious for that. Researchers are, in any case, at last beginning to be aware of the amount of physical violence of which women are the initiators.

In fact, many of our ideas about the exploitatory side of the marriage relationship are based on fixed 19th century stereotypes which no longer exist or are no longer applicable as cases in point. The French *haut bourgeois* stereotype in particular, as enshrined, for example, in the pages of Balzac and De Maupassant, has had an extraordinary longevity in popular art and people's imaginations, but much that was essential to it, including the property arrangements, the greater worldliness of men and the comparative ignorance and ductility of women, is as dead as the dodo. Indeed as far as Ireland is concerned, much of it never had any existence at all; and as things currently stand the law relating to property and maintenance, or at least the application of that law, if it can be said to favour anybody, favours the women rather than the men.

The truth is really, though, that almost any relationship between people (even two people) is impossible in our society which does not involve exploitation of some sort, even mutual exploitation, and marriage is no exception to this rule. It will also, for both parties, continue to be a trap until they are made economically independent of each other by bringing about full employment for everybody, male and female, married and unmarried; for only mutual economic independence can really make it what it ought to be, a continuing and free choice, and enable people to walk away from each other without subsequent beggary and bitterness. In present-day Ireland, the liberal cry for divorce is a mockery of people's actual situations; and to ally it, as one rather silly woman candidate in the Eurovision elections did, with the call for legalised abortion and contraception, is probably only to delay the advent of these desperately needed rights in law. Divorce in Ireland would be, like the famous annulments, a luxury for upper suburbia.

Since, however, the employment possibilities in our society are rapidly diminishing rather than increasing, the sort of employment for everybody, male and female, married and unmarried, which would end the degrading economic dependence of one party on another is not likely to come about. What may just happen, though, is that even our politicians will, in order to avert revolution, have to begin to examine the possibility of abandoning present concepts of employment in favour of a national minimum wage payable to everybody whether they are technically employed or not.

If that comes to be the case a hard and bitter fight may well lie ahead for the inclusion of everybody, young and old, married and unmarried, male and female, self-employed artists, disemployed workers and school leavers, girls included, who have technically never worked at all; for of course the politicians would try to restrict payment to fathers of families and other outmoded categories.

One way or another, though, it is only through concepts like this that the liberation of women, like the liberation of everybody else, can come about. To wage the struggle on the present level of mere equality of opportunity, pay and conditions for the more fortunate in the sort of society we have is not only to condemn it to being a mere sectional, advantage-seeking, middle-class movement (just another middle-class ramp, in fact. But it is also to ally it with what are, or ought to be by now, thoroughly discredited attitudes to education and job opportunities and to that altogether evil alliance of educationalist and employer which has destroyed imagination in every field and made self-fulfilment for the majority of people a chimera.

For the liberation of women, like every other sort mooted, is a matter of self-fulfilment and creative development in the end or it is nothing. And that this is largely a question of the economic re-organisation of society is a truth so obvious that it is difficult to see how some sisters have failed to grasp it. So is the sad fact that even the illusory and, on the whole, boring forms of self-fulfilment and creative development on offer in our society cannot be brought about except for sectional interests among women (the rich, the "educated", etc.) without abolishing sectional interests altogether, without in fact liberating all humanity.

You cannot, for example, abolish traditional concepts of what constitutes gainful or reward-worthy employment for women without abolishing them for men too. Which is something we will have to do in the very near future if we are to avoid mass mayhem, pillage and rapine.

That the sexes have a stake in each other's liberation is something that was suggested at the beginning. Of course there are in each one of us yearnings for domination and possession, products of our upbringing and training in a property-owning and exploitatory society, which go very deep. We are none of us, as Karl Marx said of himself, fit citizens of the new world. But although these things exist, and perhaps can exist at the centre of each being, what was said at the beginning is true of women no less than of men. It is, in the main, immensely more rewarding to be the lover or the friend of a free man than of a servant or a wage slave, and it is better for a woman to be the daughter of such a man too. Liberation is not a matter that you can split up between the sexes; though of course to some extent you can split it up between the classes.

Onward, Sisters, Onward

THE WOMEN have been on the rampage for some considerable time now, and the truth is that they have achieved very little. Even in terms of the objectives of quite moderate libbers, things have not progressed very far — hereabouts anyway.

When his occasions and necessities take him into the places where the great and serious work of the world is done — Radio Telefís Éireann for example — the present writer can see at a glance that the men still have nearly all the good jobs. Vast numbers of women are of course employed as menials in such places — sorting and arranging things, stalling on the telephone, making tea and coffee and performing the tasks that a computerised elctronic typing and filing system could do for one tenth of the money. But nearly everywhere the jobs that are called "responsible" — that is, the well-paid ones, the amusing ones, the ones that confer power and a feeling of self-importance on the holder — are still held by men. Equality of job opportunity, equality of status, equality of reward are still myths.

Nor, by and large, have their objectives in any other field — here in the Republic at least — been achieved. It is true that divorce and contraception, even perhaps legalised abortion, are not or ought not to be, specifically Women's Lib objectives: come to that, nothing in the way of freedom, justice or common sense ought to be specifically a Women's Lib objective. But whatever about divorce, women have quite evidently a bigger stake in contraception and abortion than men have, and they are failing pretty dismally to get either of them on the statute book.

That is to say, those women who are interested or vocal enough to be involved are failing, which means in fact very few. Enthusiasm for either divorce or legalised abortion is certainly not rampant among the daughters of Éireann; and even on the subject of contraceptive devices and their availability they are, one might (if the word hadn't changed its meaning) say, cool. Our statesmen can therefore claim with some justice that they are doing no more than reflecting the will, or at least the apathy, of the people, females included, in their refusal to give a lead or to go to the political stake over any such issues.

And there is of course a school of thought which claims that women are in any case inherently more conservative than men, particularly on issues which touch the stability of the home and family, or which have to do with sexual behaviour in all its aspects. More especially in tradition-orientated places like Ireland, say the upholders of this view, women will always be found on the side of things as they are; on the side of the priests and the Ten Commandments and repressive morality.

They may occasionally take advantage of the fact that some rather dubious changes in the family law have been handed to them on a plate. They may even agitate in a mild sort of a way for more pay, jobs and opportunities. But deep down they know which side their bread is buttered on, and they view change with suspicion. Women's Lib is therefore one of those liberal rackets whose adherents make a lot of noise without really commanding much support from the allegedly oppressed multitude on whose behalf they claim to speak. It is even a sort of coup d'etat carried out against the wishes of women themselves.

If all this were indeed true, it would be a poor lookout for those who believe that the whole repressive set-up in most human societies to date was an expression of male authoritarianism and that it was high time women began to redress the balance. And a poor lookout as well for those who hope that women's liberation will be an instrument of liberation for us all. Oddly enough, though, many of those who take the view that women are natural conservatives seem to be able to combine it with another which suggests that the real nature of women is dangerous and subversive. From the book of Genesis down to James Joyce (perhaps ironically) the authors of male literature have suggested almost unanimously that women were mischief-makers who caused nothing but trouble; that their impulses and ambitions were almost always perverse and destructive; and that it was essential for the proper functioning and ordering of society to keep them in their place.

"Women," said Rabelais, who took this view, "never bend their subtle, stubborn and contrary minds except towards what they know is prohibited or forbidden." And since most of what was prohibited or forbidden was so because men in their wisdom had decided that it was essential for the good order and continued wellbeing of society to prohibit or forbid it, this meant that the real impulses of women were a constant threat which might bring about calamity at any stage, as they already had done in the Garden of Eden, in the city of Troy and in holy Ireland at the time of Dermot McMurrough.

The two views are of course incompatible, and yet the same sort of males hold them, particularly priests and politicians. Women are natural conservatives, who can be trusted to hold things together when men get perverse and flighty; and women are destroyers who have to be watched and thwarted at every turn.

In the opinion of the present writer the second view is the more correct one. Women are inherently far more anarchic than men, far more adventurous — mischievous if you like — far less convinced than men are that the boring, uncreative and hierarchical ways in which we organise things are heaven-sent and must be maintained at all costs. The reason many women appear to be otherwise, to be, like Mrs Thatcher and a number of the dear old ladies you meet everyday, living embodiments of the repressive principle is that just as there are tall women and short women, stupid and intelligent women, so there are conservatives of that sex as well as subversives; and women are, unlike men, inclined to go to extremes. But it is also, of course, appallingly possible to become the psychic model of your oppressor, and this is what a number of women do, becoming more conservative than the House of Lords, more pietistic than the priests, more warlike than the soldiers and so on.

And women have also been conditioned for countless millions of ages to do their subversive work in secret and with specifically female weapons, attacking usually those institutions and concepts which were nearest at hand and which men held most dear: chivalry, honour, the performance principle, monogamous marriage, the laws of inheritance and primogeniture. Having been conditioned to avoid head-on confrontation, it is as difficult for them as it is for artists to convince themselves that public action is the only action that in the long run counts. Vanessa Redgraves (or Nell McCaffertys) are as rare among women as Brechts are among artists.

This may account, in part at least, for the tardiness with which women are becoming liberated everywhere, but there is, the present writer believes, one other factor in the situation which is insufficiently recognised. Large numbers of women are more aware than men are of the gap that separates our possible lives from the lives that society insists we should lead. They know that when it comes to any form of liberation whatever, we are psychically light years ahead of the society in which our lot is cast, and this knowledge has been with them probably since that revealing encounter in the Garden. But they have been encouraged and misled into thinking of liberation in terms of advantage in our kind of society, in terms merely of "getting their snouts in the trough."

The emphasis in many instances can be seen to be subtly misplaced, but in that subtle misplacement can be glimpsed a long perpetuation of our present values. To put a certain sort of emphasis on contraception, for example, is to give a tacit approval to male ideas of sexuality. To put a certain sort of emphasis on individual opportunity is to affirm that individual opportunity, the classic male bourgeois panacea for everything, is what it is all about. To put a certain sort of emphasis on getting a share of somebody's property is to agree that the possession of property is the name of the game.

Of course it is. But it may be because women are so aware of the gap which separates these things from the forms of liberation we all know to be psychically and even circumstantially possible, that they have not unleashed the full powers of their wills and energies on objectives which are at best somewhat dull and at worst atrociously limited.

Kept in Idleness

THE PRACTICE of paying people not to work is not new. Almost from the beginning of urban society, there were doles and handouts of one kind or another. At the height of things in Rome, about a quarter of a million people were in daily receipt of free food or hard cash; all work ceased at noon; and more than half the days in the year were in any case public holidays on which no work at all was done.

In the Catholic Middle Ages, a vast horde of monks, friars, nuns, priests, palmers and mendicants of all descriptions was supported at the public expense; and they in their turn supported others who were in need of Christian charity. Aristocrats kept armies of retainers and hangers-on, for martial and prestige reasons; and as ruder times gave way to more affluent, the courts of the central monarchs became places of converse and resort for large numbers of elegant people whose aristocratic disdain for work was a proof of high breeding.

With the advent of capitalism, however, came the Protestant work ethic. Not only did the new system need a labour force, but it needed one reduced to desperation and eager for any kind of work that might be offered. Enclosure of the common lands and the turning adrift of hundreds of thousands of monastic servants and aristocratic retainers provided Henrician and Elizabethan England with a huge reserve of unemployed; incredibly savage measures against idleness and vagabondage, as well as the shutting down of all the traditional centres of charitable support, ensured its demoralisation. At the same time, the idea of working for a living – of doing a fair day's work for a fair day's pay – was elevated to a moral height which it had never previously occupied in humanity's consciousness.

Some 7,200 persons were hung in England in the reign of Henry VIII for alleged thievery and tens of thousands more were branded and flogged for mere idleness and vagabondage. "And then also," wrote Thomas More, "they be cast in prison as vagabonds, because they go about and work not: whom no man will set at work, though they never so willingly proffer themselves thereto." In succeeding centuries, charity was kept to a dour minimum; the poor and the unemployed were actively persecuted and harried merely for being so; and in Britain in the nineteenth century the attitude which dictated such policies reached its logical conclusion in the new Poor Law, the first measure with which the "enlightened" Whigs celebrated their victory over aristocratic reaction in 1832 (extended to Ireland in 1838). This meant simply that if you were in need of charity or relief you would have to go into a workhouse to get it; and though you would be kept alive there you would be treated in such a manner as to remind you always that destitution and failure to obtain employment were crimes. You wore dress which amounted to prison dress; you were denied all pleasures, including the company of the opposite sex; and your attitude to the authorities and to society in general was expected to be a mixture of gratitude and shame.

Well, as we all know, Lloyd George, an unscrupulous Welsh solicitor of few convictions and immense eloquence, altered all that. Faced for the first time with Parliamentary opposition from the left in the shape of the new Labour Party and frightened by the new militant trade unionism of the 1900s, the Liberal Government of 1906 brought in a series of swift measures which established Old Age Pensions (of 5s a week for people over seventy whose income did not exceed £21 a year) and at long last Unemployment Insurance.

And no legislative innovation had been the cause of more self-congratulation in our time than these measures, and their extension and improvement. Because of our social legislation, we are supposedly more enlightened than our ancestors and not only more enlightened but more Christian as well, though the established Churches had nothing to do with the 1911 acts and even the nonconformist ones were more concerned with making it difficult for the working class to obtain drink.

We are also supposed to be somehow more socialist and more radical, though even in 1906 the radicalism of these measures diverted attention from the falling wages and rising prices which ensured that the standard of living of the workers was lower on the eve of the Great War than it had been in the closing years of the nineteenth century; while the fact is that right-wing and reactionary regimes (including Franco's) have almost as good a record where social insurance is concerned than supposedly liberal, radical or even socialist ones. It was Bismarck's Germany, not Lloyd George's Britain, which pioneered social legislation in Europe. By the acts of 1883 and 1889, the Iron Chancellor managed not only to steal the thunder of the socialists but to introduce into the German worker's consciousness an illusion of partnership in capitalist enterprise which has lasted to this day; and Hitler's record where social insurance was concered was just as good as anybody else's (which facts should be a lesson to all those who think social legislation is the name of the socialist game).

The truth is that humanitarian reasons count for very little where social legislation in the highly industrialised countries is concerned. Bismarck in the eighteen-eighties was defusing the threat of revolution in an advanced country with a high degree of Marxist consciousness; and all the governments of Europe have seen the logic of his policies since. In these islands in recent years, doles have been gladly enough paid out because a high level of not very lavishly subsidised unemployment has been a delightful bonus for governments who, having themselves created and abetted inflationary situations, were forced by their German and American masters to become concerned about them.

Unemployment both induces moderation of demand among the employed, and is itself deflationary since the dole does not keep pace with living costs and will certainly not run ahead of them. Consequently, the payment of it has been a cross which our governments (or, to be more precise, their world banking partners) have been very glad to bear.

Still, in spite of the evident necessity for the payment of such doles and subsidies to large numbers of unemployed and the fact that they are likely to become a permanent feature of capitalist life, society as we know it has remained very uneasy about their existence, and has approached them much more hypocritically than did the Romans. At first sight this might seem to be due to the fact that the work ethic was a real one which took a real grip; but on the other hand, even post-Reformation middle-class society never saw anything wrong with subsidised idleness provided it was the prerogative of those who had established a claim to it by greed, acquisitiveness and control of the law.

Those authors, such as our own poor Oliver Goldsmith, who spoke for the eighteeenth century middle class were full of disdain for the idle aristocrat. But as soon as the middle classes had themselves achieved rentier status, they, like their aristocratic predecessors began to claim that the existence of idle (or as they would have put it, leisured) ladies and gentlemen was essential to the progress of civilisation.

So indeed it was; but nobody speaks like that nowadays about the unemployed; and though we have begun to hear more and more about some sort of mythical "education for leisure" which is supposed to begin to transform things the probable pattern for the future is already well established. Everybody, including the trade unions (which will represent only those lucky enough to remain in employment through all the technological changes) will hang on to such advantages as they may have. The unemployed will become a sub-class whose depredations and vandalisms will be controlled as far as possible by segregation and ghettoisation in "depressed areas."

Neither the fruits of technology, nor work, nor leisure will be shared out with any semblance of equality; for even if our advantage-ridden society had the will, it could not within the present vested interest structure of things find the means. The notion of an educated populace, sensitive to art and literature and with plenty of time to enjoy them, will continue to remain a dream of schoolmasters, suburban housewifes, debating society members and the sort of people who write letters to the editor.

December 1978

Time on Our Hands

WHATEVER THE published forecasts say, it is now perfectly clear that the unemployment figures for the early eighties will be quite staggering; that the present trend is irreversible; and that in western Europe at least, something like a third or more of the active population will fairly soon be out of work.

It is also perfectly clear that nobody in authority is devoting any real thought to the matter; that the conservative forces in our society, including the trade unions, will continue to ensure that those who are fortunate enough to be working will retain the advantage over those who are not; and that to be unemployed will be to suffer both psychologically and financially in much the same way as it is today.

And in these circumstances, it is going to be difficult for even the clearest-headed amongst us to remember that the silicon chip is not a visitation from on high, a twentieth-century equivalent of brimstone or bubonic plague; but instead a boon and a blessing to men as important and potentially at least as liberating as the wheel, the hose collar, the iron plough and the steam engine.

Yet that is what indeed it is; and to say otherwise is a form of blasphemy against the human attributes which are specifically god-like: creativity, ingenuity, the indomitable will to pursue knowledge and bend nature to our own ends.

For there is no virtue whatever in doing something the hard way when you can in fact do it the easy. There is no virtue either in doing something useless, irrelevant and dull when you could be doing something exciting, creative or beneficial to your fellows. And there is still less virtue in squandering the most precious asset human beings have – to wit, their time – when they could be using it in fruitful or purposeful ways.

It may even be rather jolly to go to the office and chat and brew tea in the intervals of typing up the reports and forms that an inexpensive computerised system could dispose of in half the time with one tenth of the workforce. Everybody sitting at home idle, whether in the suburban box, the furnished room or the corporation flat knows that work, however irrelevant or superfluous it may be in some ultimate scheme of things, is not necessarily the worst option. But at the same time, when one machine can do ten typists' work, where previously, as my learned colleague Keith

Waterhouse says in a cross-Channel publication, it took ten girls to do one typist's work, then not to use it is an abysmal confession that most human beings find life pointless and purposeless, that the thing they most dread is having time on their hands, and that if they weren't herded into work in the mornings and kept there for most of their waking hours, the knowledge of the void would become unbearable and existence itself a burden.

Of course let us admit that, as things stand, for the compulsorily idle, it very often is. Many people, in our society, do not know how to use their time. Many are as totally devoid of mental or spiritual resource as a billiard ball is of hair. And for most, in our society, to be idle is to be in one degree or another cut off from the company of one's fellows, from comradeship and any feeling of communal satisfaction.

"If you are idle, be not solitary, if you are solitary, be not idle," was the advice Samuel Johnson gave Boswell about beating the blues; but most people in our society who are condemned to idleness are condemned to a lowering amount of solitude at the same time. Our present form of social organisation neither encourages, desires, nor educates for self-sufficiency; and except for alcoholism, unending rounds of golf and the daytime television, it has nothing to put in the place of the satisfactions (or pseudo-satisfactions) and comradeships (or fake fellowships) of the factory or the office.

The problem therefore is twofold. We must find, individually and collectively, exciting, useful and rewarding things to do with the time we are going to have on our hands. And we must find a method or methods of either sharing the products of our labours, or, better still, the labours themselves, so that the present horrible, heartrending and, in any case, utterly outdated distinction between employed and unemployed is abolished.

And make no mistake about it, the second one is going to be both the most important and the trickiest. To the conservative, the greedy and the stupid, the notion of a share-out, of yielding up advantages and giving people something for nothing, is always an abomination. Advantage-seeking, greed and the work-ethic, all of which are bred into our very bones, combine to make it a strange one to us all; and at the top or towards the top, there are those who know the vast profits to be reaped from the new technology provided it is used, like all the technologies before it, for profit and not for liberation. While so long as national units remain, it will be dinned into us that we must compete not only with our neighbours but with our fellow-men all over the earth; and that the secret of successful competition is to use the new technology as "efficiently" as possible — which means, as always, with a payroll as small as possible and profits just as high.

Yet, one way or another, the technology itself will brook neither denial nor delay. The most likely outcome of all the possible outcomes is that when the numbers of unemployed under the present system have risen sufficiently high there will be a bust-up, and that instead of a rational and properly-managed transition to something else, we will have a nasty, dangerous and revengeful one.

On the other hand, large numbers of people have now had a sufficient glimpse of possibility to make them impatient and the feeling that we are stupidly mis-managing a collective opportunity is growing. In the diffused socialistic feelings so widespread among so many, we can even see the technology itself creating a new ethos which may well triumph in spite of our worser, meaner and more old-fashioned selves. As the man said, when men change their mode of production they change their ideas. "The hand mill will give you a society with the fuedal lord, the steam mill a society with the industrial capitalist." And the silicon chip . . .?

The Hard Facts

OVER THE last decade or so Irish history has, in the interests of a certain sort of persuasion, been, it is not too much to say, re-written, with certain of its realities de-emphasised in favour of others. Thus the Tudor conquest of Ireland becomes a matter of England's strategic necessities, which it was; but it almost ceases to be a matter of brutal colonial extirpation, which it also was.

And the de-emphasisation goes on. In the course of some contributions to this newspaper about the relationship of Britain and Ireland, Father Joseph Dunn, a former director of the Catholic Communications Institute, who now works with Radharc Films and the Research and Development Commission of the Hierarchy, said:

> In the days of Britain's greatness as a world power, it was politically inconceivable for her to leave Ireland open to the meddling influence of other powers. In those days no great power could afford to have potential enemies at large in its backyard. The British attempt to control and pacify Ireland over so many centuries was a tragedy for Ireland. But given the facts of history, England had to be in Ireland. The fault lies as much in geographical position as in any particular quirks of the British people.

The argument is, more or less, that it was all strategy and self-preservation. The counter-argument is implied to be that the "British people" were power-hungry conquerors by disposition and character. There is not a word said about plain, ordinary, honest-to-god economic exploitation. Not a word about classes or greed.

Now to say that the marcher barons left Pembrokeshire for strategic reasons in the first place would of course be plainly ridiculous. They came to Ireland with their armoured horsemen and their archers trained in the Welsh wars for the same reasons that, a couple of generations before, their forebears had come to England: for land and loot, for territory and all that went with it.

You could on the other hand argue that, they having come, their feudal overlord Henry II had little option but to come after them, if it were not for the fact that as far back as 1155 he had begun to make diplomatic and other preparations for invasion. He took exactly the same step as his predecessor, William the Conqueror had before invading England: that is, he secured approval from the Supreme Pontiff for the enterprise. Still, except for the fact that certain members of the Anglo-Norman-Welsh ruling class had struck it lucky in the new land, and that there were opportunities for profitable trade out of the Pale area into Britain, the partial conquest of Ireland was undoubtedly of small economic importance to anybody until Tudor times. Then the story is different.

No-one but a lunatic would suggest that given the international situation and the long rivalry with Spain, the total subjugation of Ireland was not a matter of real strategic importance to the British Crown. Nor indeed that as far back as the reign of Henry VII, the existence of a turbulent and semi-independent nobility, many of them Yorkists, and inclined, in Henry VII's words, "to crown apes" such as Lambert Simnel or Perkin Warbeck, was not a matter of concern to the new Tudor dynasty. It was against the tide of the times. But on the other hand it is nonsense to suggest that the late Tudor conquest did not have an economic dimension; that the economic stakes were not high and the profits enormous.

Nor was colonial conquest, as understood by the Elizabethans and Jacobeans, a matter of trade with and exploitation of the pacified natives. Imperialist theory did not run to that in the later sixteenth century. No more than in the matter of the Indians of North America did Elizabethan colonial entrepreneurs see the Irish as possible, if unequal, trading partners or sheep for the fleecing. Their mere presence was a nuisance on all counts; and it was on the final desirability of getting rid of them altogether that the best brains among those which were weighing the strategic problems in later Elizabethan times, and those who were moved by mere greed, came together.

Through plain confiscation, the discovery of defective title, the demand for unpaid Crown rents and other devices, large areas were made available. The hope was that they would be cleared entirely of the natives who encumbered them and populated instead by a cross-section of English society: gentlemen, freeholders, tenant farmers, craftsmen, shopkeepers, tenants and labourers. When the Desmond estates and the lands of one hundred and forty others were confiscated in Munster (Sir Walter Raleigh, for example, receiving in the end about 80,000 acres) official circulars were sent out through Justices of the Peace all over England and Government officials went round the country urging the advantages of settlement in the new colony on all classes of the populace.

And, in spite of occasional setbacks and the periodic need of Stuart monarchs to find allies and armies among the native Irish, total clearance and resettlement may be said to have been the main plank in British policy towards Ireland for almost the next hundred years: until, in fact, there was almost nothing left to grant or re-grant. If total clearance and re-settlement had not by then been achieved, it was only because it was a shining but unattainable ideal in the first place and was sabatoged by the greed which moved the larger grantees to cheat or keep out the smaller. Cromwellian officers and the financiers who had received grants against Civil War loans cheated and kept out Cromwellian common soldiers, or made life so impossible for them that they were glad to go home and leave their lands to the larger man. And that these larger men somehow became Irish because they had Irish estates, so that England ceased to be connected with their profits or behaviour, is a fiction — a polite one, but still a fiction.

Ireland was the booty of the victorious class (largely a middle class, which is maybe why they made poor aristocrats) in two English civil wars, of the financiers who backed the right side and of the possibly malcontent winning soldiery. Its strategic importance to England was not negligible; and neither was the role it played as a recruiting ground and otherwise in an English power struggle; but the economic advantages of conquest were as real as the top-boots of the conquerors.

After the final Williamite Acts of Settlement and Explanation had, in accordance with the moderate tone of the regime, done their best to satisfy all the parties to the English quarrels, there were less than two million statute acres (out of over twelve million) in the hands of Irish or old English landowners and there was no more land-booty to be got. For the next century or so, the chief economic advantage of the conquest, apart from rents (which our new historians are inclined to forget, the landlords from now on being "Irish") was in Ireland as a source of cheap food and raw materials. Whenever Ireland looked like becoming anything else, England, in Karl Marx's words, "struck down the manufacture of Ireland, depopulated her cities and threw the people back upon the land."

From time to time, the kind of food or the kind of raw material that was wanted might change, but with the coming of the Industrial Revolution Ireland became the vitally important source of a hitherto (except for military reasons) neglected commodity; human beings. So great was the importance of Ireland as a source of cheap, uprooted and demoralised labour that it is doubtful if the English Industrial Revolution could have taken place without it. Without the endemic conditions and the appalling calamities that drove the Irish to crowd into the basements and hovels of the new English towns, to compete with the English working-class and undermine its first efforts to secure better conditions, the whole history of Britain in the cotton and railway age would have been different.

The first requisite for an industrial revolution is a labour force. Enclosure and the reorganisation of agriculture were providing one in Britain, at a frightful human cost. But as Hobsbaum says, "the forces tending to prize men loose from their historic social anchorage were still relatively weak" before 1848; and "it took a really sensational catastrophe such as the Irish hunger to produce the sort of massive emigration which became common after 1850."

After the Act of Union the English mercantilism which had crippled Irish industry for most of the eighteenth century had been replaced by unhindered English competition, a much more deadly affair. Hobsbaum's description of pre-Famine Ireland is an accurate one:

> Except in the north-East (Ulster) the country had long been deindustrialised by the mercantilist policy of the British government whose colony it was, and more recently by the competition of British industry. A single technical innovation – the substitution of the potato for the previously prevalent types of farming – had made a large increase in population possible . . . Since there was no alternative employment – for industrialisation was excluded – the end of this evolution was mathematically predictable. Once the population had grown to the limits of the last potato patch, carved out of the last piece of just-cultivable bog, there would be a catastrophe.

After the Famine and the repeal of the Corn Laws, horned cattle, wool and human beings became the principal commodities that the English economy (of which Ireland was a part) demanded. So the depopulation of rural Ireland became the enlightened policy, being most persuasively advocated by, among others, Lord Dufferin, the son of the lady who wrote "The Emigrant's Farewell". Of course numbers of absentees continued to draw rent and the middlemen and the newer landlord class continued to invest the profits of Irish land-holding in England as well as in churches. (Throughout the century Irish investment in England was, whatever they may say about the Act of Union now, a not inconsiderable factor in England's prosperity). As T.P. O'Connor twigged at the time, the Land Acts were originally designed to give the landlord class a smaller but more stable income and what amounted to legal permission to be absentees. The rest, including Balfour's establishment of a backward, conservative peasant class as the primary class in Ireland, we know.

But, Father Dunn may say (at least everybody else seems to be saying) what is the point of rehearsing it all now? Why not, in the words of the once popular song, let bygones be bygones? The answer is, in part, that we are not yet done with England and with the whole English-created syndrome; and that we have to get our historical situation sorted out before we can understand or can do anything whatsoever.

It is not contended that numbers of people in Ireland would not have been subject to economic misfortune and exploitation if England had never been heard of. But an agreement or a conspiracy to deny, or even to play down, the fact that the British ruling classes exploited this country with their hearts' content for over three hundred years and made, for much of the time, a more or less deliberate attempt to depopulate it can surely do nobody at all any good. If we have had one false, over-simplified version of history foisted on us, let us for heaven's sake not be saddled with another one now.

The Republican Dilemma

ON MAY 10th, 1795, seventy-two secretly elected delegates met in convention in Belfast. Their aim was to re-constitute the Society of United Irishmen, formed originally in 1791; but in the policy of the new organisation there was to be a shift of emphasis so great as to constitute an altogether new departure. The membership oath of the old body had spoken of "the attainment of an impartial and adequate representation of the Irish nation in Parliament." On this occasion the business concluded by the chairman asking each delegate a formal question as to what he stood for and receiving from each an expected answer. It was: "A republican government and separation from England."

From the beginning the new organisation faced a difficulty which has been endemic in Irish republicanism ever since. It consisted mostly of artisans, small shopkeepers and farmers who had been influenced by the ideas of the French Revolution. As time went by there was a marked accretion of middle-class intellectuals who had been similarly swayed by events in France. All were independent enough or clear-headed enough not to have been deterred by the "atrocities" and "excessess" of the French Jacobins.

They believed quite genuinely in liberty, equality and fraternity. Superstitition of any kind and religious intolerance of all shades were anathema to them. To that extent their thinking was, and must surely still be accounted, progressive. But their thinking was, all the same, the thinking of intellectuals; and they had no mass following.

It was essential that the new United Ireland Society should link itself in some way with the people's hopes; but, what was perhaps even more important, and, as time was to show, rendered it vulnerable in important ways, it had to link itself also with their fears and discontents. To do this its founders had to establish contact with a network of organisations in many ways more powerful but vastly more shadowy in substance and confused in its objectives than their own. These were the Defender societies which owed their existence, as the Whiteboys before them had done, to intolerable local grievances and burdens, matters of life and death which, on the local level, appeared to be very remote from the debates of the Convention or the principles enshrined by Tom Paine.

In so far as they were to effect a linkage the United Irishmen had to become the representatives of these resentments and fears. But the immediate enemies of the peasantry — the landlord, the parson who received the iniquitous tithe, very likely the landgrabber — were Protestants; and so was the whole establishment behind them, right up to the Castle clique who controlled the militia and all the apparatus of oppression. There was therefore very little that the peasantry could do, either in the way of self-defence or attack, that was not in some definition of the word, and in practice if not in specific intention, sectarian.

In the north-east corner of Ireland itself, the real home of the new republicanism, sectarian animosities were in fact arriving at a new degree of bitterness and in the very year of the Society's foundation came to a bloody climax in the famous battle of the Diamond at Armagh, the result of an especially savage and extensive Orange pogrom. If the peasantry were to strike, or to strike back, it almost had to be at Protestants of one kind or another. Given the actual circumstances of life among the Catholic masses it was inevitable that they should translate the dream of liberty and the principles of revolution into sectarian, that is, into religious terms. The root and base of the oppression appeared to them to be religious. The oppression personified, whether in military or in clerical garb was, ninety-nine times in a hundred, religious. And in these circumstances it proved apallingly easy for the government to play on Protestant fears.

In return, the United Irishmen played on Catholic fears. Engaged though they were in a struggle for a glorious, non-sectarian republic, it was in part a question of the end justifying the means. So whatever their principles, there is, alas, no doubt that they spread rumours where they could of an impending massacre of all Catholics by the Protestant and Orange elements. Castlereagh described the Wexford outbreak as; "a Jacobin conspiracy with Popish instruments" and to some extent this was true. The result was that when finally the Protestant and Orange-officered militia succeeded in goading the people of Wexford beyond endurance (giving of course a very real substance to their fear that a religious war had been declared against them while they did so) much that happened was a stain on the annals of liberty itself. Scullabogue was in part at least, the result of republicanism, with all its non-sectarian principles. In the new hope and the new dream there was, for the time being anyway, the seed of the old horror.

But, of course if Scullabogue was, in that sense, the result of the first Irish republicanism, it was equally the result of the fact that there was, in Ireland, a power which had a vested interest in religious hatred and conflict, and which was always masked by the instrument which was, in one sense or another, also its victim. Reporting to his superiors that he was starting a search for arms in the vicinity, the commander of Dungannon wrote:

> And this I do, not so much with a hope to succeed to any extent, as to increase the animosity between the Orangemen and the United Irishmen ... Upon that animosity depends the safety of the entire counties of the North.

Still, it meant, and since the circumstances have always been more or less analogous, it has continued to mean, that Irish republicanism has always been to some extent on the horns of a dilemma. The masses' preoccupations were not always, or not in any real sense, republican. Defenderism has always been as much a part of their motivation as has the tolerant, true republicanism of Wolfe Tone, Robert Emmet and Thomas Clarke Luby. And to the precise extent that Defenderism, with all its confusions and errors and excesses, its racial and religious overtones, has been a principal factor in any given movement, so have other elements been alienated.

From the time when the original Francophile revolutionaries and intellectuals reached out to gain support among those who were caught in the dreary vicious cycle of deprivation, fear and revenge leading to further racial and religious conflict, so did other Presbyterians, or, for that matter, Deistic liberals, repudiate them and the movement they had bred. And to that precise extent also did the Defender psychology gain control frequently of the Republican movement itself.

And this psychology has many manifestations, not always so overtly repugnant to republican principles as might appear. A cool reappraisal of Irish history since 1795 might show that republicanism has played a rather smaller part in it than many people assume; and whatever Noel Browne may say about our present ills, it is doubtful if, from the time of the Mansion House committee on, republicanism was really the dominant force in the separatist movement that led eventually to the Treaty and the 1937 Constitution. There are more or less intellectual Defenders as well as the more benighted, the more ignorant or the more desperate kind; and much of our separatism has been compounded of Catholic and racial elements which have little to do with the ideals of Emmet and Tone. But whatever its terminology, Defenderism is always the product of fear and insecurity: fear, even, perhaps, for what is conceived to be "race" itself and its physical and cultural survival: an important aspect of the psychology of many of the leaders of the post-1916 period, de Valera very much included.

Leaving "race" out of it, sometimes these fears have been well grounded, so well grounded, indeed, that the heart goes out to the fearful and their conservator or conservative leaders. In '98, for example, the people were truly desperate and in Belfast in more recent times it is easy to understand why the Defender psychology should sometimes have been paramount over the Republican ideology.

The failure perhaps lies in the failure of republicanism to translate into a true, open mass-movement with the support from every section which its separatist but truly libertarian principles deserve. Part of its tragedy is that it has always had to operate conspiratorially on a stage set by its opponents. The dilemma which has been described, though at times more acute than at others, is a real one, but, of course, it did not come into existence of its own accord. At the precise moment that Republicanism was born the trap was so cunningly set that a despairing view of Irish history might suggest that it was inescapable.

Up the Republic!

THE LATE Patrick Kavanagh used to say that "republicanism was a Protestant invention: it had little to do with the Irish people." In its accuracy as well as its bold disregard for nuance and scruple in the matter of who the Irish people precisely are, the statement is worth bearing in mind. Certainly it is true in its first part. Republicanism was a Protestant invention, or a Protestant import. And if by the Irish people is meant (as undoubtedly the speaker meant) the aboriginal, Catholic element who compose the majority of the population, it is true in its second part also.

Republicanism had, in its origins, little enough to do with them. It has always been but accidentally related to their foremost wishes and desires. In its long history only Robert Emmet, who had a gift for association and comradeship with all classes and forms of intellectual development, brought it anywhere near being a true mass movement, and then only among the Dublin working class. As a principle and cause it has never sat easily upon the farming element, although the landless poor and the disinherited by primogeniture have been more attracted to it than others. And the urban Catholic middle class has always disliked it, secretly or otherwise; demanded dilution of its doctrine when it was adopted as a slogan, and found more than one historic occasion to desert it and betray it.

And the reasons for this are not really far to seek. The first republicans were indeed Protestants by origin and upbringing, but in their thought and their attitudes they were freethinkers, or at best Deists. The source of their ideas and of the hopes that came so easily to them in that optimistic dawn was the French Revolution.

By the time these ideas found organisational form in Ireland the Bastille had been stormed; the hated Civil Constitution had been imposed upon the French clergy; and Louis XVI and Marie Antoinette had fled to Varennes and been brought back to face the wrath of the people. It was understood by the more perceptive of reactionaries in Ireland by then (and even though they have used the name of the Republic often enough since it is still understood by them) that the Republic was secular or it was nothing. If it had been nothing else but secular it would have had the Catholic Church against it, for that Church was beginning to recognise that it had encountered in French republicanism a force such as it had never encountered before in human affairs, a fact it has never forgotten, distant though the French Revolution may seem to some of us. And it would, of course, have had against it too all those who knew in their bones that religion was their prop and stay in worldly matters, including the "oppressed" Catholic middle-classes.

But although the true republican ideal was secular and is secular, it was, even then, much more. Even as early as the summer of 1791, when, although Brissot and the Girondins appeared triumphant in France, the Cordeliers Club had begun to interest itself in the plight of the unemployed, to give support to striking workers and to enrol wage-earners and small craftsmen in fraternal societies affiliated to the parent Club in the Rue Dauphine, Irish republicanism was astonishingly advanced and radical in its outlook. It was already in fraternal communication with the Jacobin Club and it was taking a very ad hoc and pragmatic view of the class structure and the relationship between classes in Ireland.

Far from being a creed for backwoodsmen, obscurantists, racists, conservationists and all those terrified of the changes implicit in the growth of knowledge and sophistication in the modern world, it was in fact radical, modernist, internationalist and of its very essence forward-looking. It stood for change and change unlimited in matters which might affect the vested interest of every tyrant conceivable, whether his sphere of operation was the schoolroom, the family circle, the workshop, the seminary or the farm. And though appearances may frequently have been to the contrary, as a living tradition, whether intellectual or practical, and a force in Irish affairs, whether with the tide, or, more often than not, against it, it continued to stand so throughout the nineteenth century. To be a republican was to be a secularist and a progressive, or it was to be a fraud.

Yet the reason things have so often appeared to be otherwise is because there are and were so many other varieties of separatism, nationalism and mere advantage-seeking on offer; because republicanism was a bold movement which in almost every generation has believed with Fintan Lalor, one of the great republicans; "that somewhere, and somehow, and by somebody a beginning must be made", because it therefore provided, time and time again, the forerunners and the martyrs; and because it has suited other people to lay claim to martyrs, forerunners, selected texts and oddly assorted principles all at once.

Professor John A. Murphy has said with truth that the primary tradition of the South is not republicanism but the "gut nationalism of a homogeneous Catholic people" which paid lip-service to republicanism, a sort of tribalism or racism which was waiting its day of victory. Though he might have pointed out how much republicanism (for after all, you cannot pay even lip-service to an ideal without being in some sort influenced by it) did to modify that tribalism when the day of victory came in this part of the island, it remains true that republicanism, or carefully selected aspects of it, has had to bear the weight not only of tribal nationalism, but of land-seeking, job-seeking, business protection-seeking and a great deal else besides.

When Patrick Pearse sought, in the great late essays which it is surely incumbent upon us to take as his mature testament, to define the republican tradition he was hard set enough to find even such a civilised, conservationist nationalist as Davis a place in it; and had to admit that Mitchel was (like himself perhaps) a late enough convert. Most of the mass movements, or pseudo-mass movements of the nineteenth century — Emancipation, Repeal, tenant right, land purchase, Home Rule — were not republican movements. And no more, in all probability, was the mass movement which appeared to frank republican doctrine with the seal of the people's approval in 1918. Republicanism has always been a fairly lonely business in Ireland, as most republicans have found out, at least until that particular generation was dead or doddering.

Then, of course, strange things would happen. And in this twentieth century, we have seen all too clearly how the posthumous appropriation of republicans and republicanism works.

Indeed Pearse himself, now in this centenary year to be rescued alike from his detractors and his admirers, may stand as the prime example of this sort of appropriation. To dispense at the same time with what Charlie Donnelly called "the gum of sentiment" and the gimcrack psychology which latter-day school-marms delight to exercise on great men, and to read his writings for what they are, is to realise that you stand in the presence of a liberal who is far more radical in his liberalism than most of those who have the name of that virtue hereabouts nowadays, and who is, on any real assessment, an enemy to be reckoned with where most sorts of oppression are concerned.

Among the many oppressed sections of the community that he was on the side of, he was fiercely on the side of children, and of the child's right to do, in a very literal sense, what he or she pleased. But a generation that grew up with the leather thongs of the Christian brothers as their birthright could scarcely have been expected to realise that unless they had come across his writings — in fact, except for the unfortunately unctuous, "Íosagán", suspiciously difficult to obtain — for themselves. All they knew was that the Christian Brothers claimed Pearse almost as a founder member. And to the whack of the thongs they heard about his piety, his purity, his idealism and his love of his poor old mother.

And who, listening to the preposterous drivel about the aim and purpose of nationality and nationhood that we were all subjected to, could have known that Patrick Pearse enunciated as his first principle that "The end of freedom is human happiness"; and as his second that "The end of national freedom is individual freedom; therefore individual happiness"? Though it is true that statements such as "nationality is a spiritual fact" have, particularly when taken out of context, an inauspicious ring for ears on the alert for proto-fascism, the centenary now approaching will do no harm at all if it enables us really to join debate at last on the republican attitudes to separatism, nationality and national union.

First then let it be said that the idea of the indivisible nation, which derived its right to be a nation from its distinguishable boundaries and its sense of collectivity, came not from the heated imagination of some racist obscurantist, but from France and French republicanism. The idea of "The Great Nation" is as integral to the Revolution as is democracy itself. And like the French republicans, whose country was in danger of being carved up and made into a second Germany from the day the Bastille was stormed until the Peace of Amiens, the Irish republicans had a very clear idea of what foreign reaction intended in the way of sectional and sectarian division in Ireland.

At the very moment of writing, the air is thick with proposals which will perpetuate and give a new gloss to the sectional divisions of our country. Every bankrupt, policyless party there is, has a constitution, federal, confederal or otherwise, in its pocket, and every tin-pot lawyer who poses as a giant intellect among his political playmates imagines himself to be the Abbé Sieyes in person and is busy adding the final phrases to a Bill of Rights to go with it.

Let it be said, then, that in the republican view a sectional division is nothing but a buttressing and a political formalisation of a sectarian division; that a sectarian division masks and aids a class division or a division along the lines of somebody's economic interest; and that such divisions are hateful as giving a foothold to foreign reaction and plausibility to our own. To encourage anybody to look for sectarian guarantees is to dignify sectarianism by making it the law of the land; to invoke an outside power or powers is to give it or them leave or licence to say how long sectarian divisions shall last in legal form.

But there is something more to the republican view and it is this. In the secular Republic — under the sane, open, unsuperstitious, or as the first Apostles would have said, enlightened secularism of the Republic, enshrined as it would be in law no other guarantee is needed by anybody, Catholic or Protestant, Mormon or Moslem, black or white, green or blue. That separation and unity are no option for those labouring under inherited fears without a guarantee that the state power would be secular in its operation, republican tradition well understood from the days of Tone to those of Thomas Clarke Luby and beyond. Yet that single negative guarantee, much more easily enshrinable in law than a lot of the mumbo-jumbo that we are about to be asked to enshrine, once given, needs no other.

The wonder is that Protestants in our time have not understood that so clearly as Tone did or many others did: but since republicanism was so very largely their creation (as well, of course, as mankind's) in the first place, there may yet be more hope for us all than we think. A Protestantism which depends on what it can snatch from temporary majorities, outside interventions and the tide of time will soon enough perhaps be dead to Ireland; but it is not dead yet.

Save Ye Kindly Ma'am

I SEE from the *Republican News* that the British Queen's visit to the north-eastern corner of this island is due to begin on Wednesday, August 10th, at 08.30 hrs. There can be little doubt about this, because the *Republican News* actually provides a photostat of the confidential documents which set out her majesty's schedule; and accordingly I can reveal that at that precise moment the Royal Yacht, Brittania, will enter Belfast Lough.

I say the British Queen so that there be no doubt about the matter. Not so long ago, the catalogue of the Jack Yeats exhibition at the National Gallery thanked "Her Majesty, the Queen" for the loan of certain pictures, thus leaving the patrons in the dark – for it could have been the Danish Queen, or the Dutch Queen, or even the Queen of Sheba who owned them. But it is the Queen of Great Britain and Northern Ireland, to give her her official style and titles, who will be making the hazardous-sounding after-breakfast transfer to HMS Fife at 10.15 and departing for Hillsborough Castle by helicopter ten mintues later, wind and weather permitting.

She will doubtless get a warm welcome, but what makes the devotion of large numbers of people in the northern part of Ireland to the British or any crown the more odd is the fact that they are Calvinist by religion. From its very beginnings, Calvinism and republicanism have gone hand in hand. Zwingli was a convinced republican on theological grounds; and almost everywhere Calvinism went, republics sprang up like tents to accomodate and shelter the preachers. Apart from the theological justifications it was natural enough that a religion which set such prime store by thrift, industry, sobriety, responsibility and the individual conscience should view monarchs and monarchial hangers-on with disfavour.

Accordingly, as soon as they obtained power, the Calvinist and Low Church elements in England were not loth to chop off the head of King Charles I. It is true that in Scotland, from which much of the present population of the northern part of Ireland originally came, there were political complications. In order to get rid of his own rightful Queen, Mary Queen of Scots – or, as he preferred to call her, Mary of Guise – John Knox sought the support of the Scottish nobility; and eventually his politics led him, as politics will, to disgrace the Calvinist faith by saddling the two islands with the absolutist King James and his blasphemous notions about the Divine right of monarchs.

It was this King James who, in the course of time, planted in Ireland most of the settlers from whom northern Calvinists trace their descent; but so little did Stuart ideas consort with theirs that within half a century of that plantation, the southern Irish and the Catholics of the north had taken up arms to defend his son's cause against the Calvinist English parliament. The total besottment of many of the southern Irish and their Catholic nobility with the monarchical principle and the Stuart cause is something well-established; but that the northern settlers, like the Tagues and bog-trotters whose ancestors supported the Stuarts, have also been from the very beginning the tools of causes not their own is a fact so glaringly obvious that it must some day dawn on them. It is true that they have enjoyed the comparatively uninterrupted tenancy or smallholdings made fertile by their own grim efforts and certain pathetic rights and privileges as an upper stratum of the proletariat; but, apart from anything else, to be condemned to a perennial limbo of provinciality in two countries is a horrible fate.

It is noteworthy that no Ulsterman of Calvinist-planter descent has ever distinguished himself in the mainstream of English/British life or has been admitted into the antechambers, let alone the councils, of the monarchs they have so fervently adored. The military caste which produced so many admired heroes was high Church and English in ethos and origin; and so have been most of the political leaders who proclaimed that Ulster would fight and Ulster would be right. Northern Irish Calvinism has not even any Flemings or Logie-Bairds, Ramsay MacDonalds or James Barries to boast of, never mind a Robert Burns. It is an inescapable conclusion that the respect for authority, for one's betters and for the hierarchies and ikons of monarchy which the unremitting propaganda of alien interests has made them believe their own, running counter as it does to the republican and levelling principles of the Calvinist religion, has been totally unsuited to their genius.

Monarchy, hierarchy and all their accompanying superstitions and snobberies are in fact much more of a Taigue thing than a northern Proddy thing. The natural division in the dark night of history in this island should have been between a royalist, intransigent south and a republican pragmatical north, with the south clinging to some ridiculous dynasty, imported or otherwise, and the north insisting on the right of a man's individual conscience and belief to be represented through individuals in Parliament. Of course the boss parliament in Ireland was always the British parliament; and the wretched Stuarts were only interested in the British crown. The reason Irish history is repetitive and irrational is that nothing indigenous was ever allowed to happen here: everything that happened had reference to somewhere else.

We never got our Stuart dynasty or succeeded in restoring any sort of native one against which the north could assert republican principle. The Hanoverian settlement in England, with its guarantees for the Protestant conscience and Protestant supremacy, and the French revolution, to which the south and the Catholics looked for liberation from Britain as they had once looked to the Bourbons, the Hapsburgs and the Pope, altered the natural balance of things. By some weird sort of inversion, the south became apparently republican as the north became allegedly monarchist.

How deep the monarchical principle went in the south, though, is amply evidenced by the mileage the poets continued to get out of it long after all possible native dynasties, and even the Stuart one, had been swept away. Eoghan Rua Ó Súilleabháin was born within five years after Cullodon and died within a similar space of time before the French Revolution; yet he wrote poems in which the beautiful maiden, when questioned, reveals that she is Erin and that the reason for her distress is that she is in mourning for her true mate who is exiled beyond the seas. Her true mate was throughout most of Eoghan Rua's short lifetime hitting the bottle hard and having alcoholic nightmares in Padua and points east. He had never set foot in Ireland, and he had cynically destroyed the Gaelic civilisation of Scotland in a desperate bid for the English throne. No matter, though. Monarchical principle dies hard in southern Ireland; and long after Eoghan Rua himself had perished from the blow that Colonel Daniel Cronin's servant struck him with the alehouse tongs, Mr. W.B. Yeats was going on about monarchy as if it was a possible option for a renascent south.

That in spite of all its snobberies and romantic, sentimental weaknesses the self-same south had not in the interval attached itself to the royal personages who sat on the British throne was due only in part to the growth of a republican ideology or to the fact that (as the recent election again proved) separatist feelings of one kind or another will always prevail over other blandishments in southern Ireland. Of not inconsiderable importance also was the fact that no died-in-the-wool romantic monarchist could possibly regard the Hanoverian and Wettin-Ernestine dynasties as other than a joke. Even the provincial snobs who focused on the Lord Lieutenant were inclined to regard him as somewhat more genuine an article than Queen Victoria, just as many people in England today think more highly of the Norfolks than they do of the royal family.

As it is, republicanism, which dates its incarnation from the meeting of Wolfe Tone and some northern Presbyterian gentlemen in Belfast at four o'clock in the afternoon of October 14th, 1791, is perhaps the only thing that north and south, Calvinist and Catholic, planters and true Gael can claim in common except Irishness. The ludicrous militarist and other flim-flam that will surround the monarch on Wednesday will be an insult, not only to the Catholic or republican element in the north, but to the Calvinist traditions and principles of the rest of the north's people as well.

Everybody knows nowadays, of course, that the monarchy has no power; and that even if her gills were interested in preserving the freedom, religion and laws of the north's Protestants in certain circumstances she could and would not lift a finger to do so. What is less often recognised is how dependence on the British monarchy, or even the Crown in Parliament, has monotonously spelled ruin for classs after class in Ireland. Where now, as people with living cultural traditions and a special contribution to make to Ireland any longer, are the Normans and Anglo-Normans, the "old English" who spent their blood and treasure for the Stuarts, the Cromwellian landlord class who turned monarchist after the Williamite settlement and repeated their devotion to Hanover through the Act of Union? Even the Protestant middle and lower-middle classes who lived in all the little Victorian streets of Dublin and put out Union Jacks on the occasion of another jubilee a mere eighty years ago? To think of them and of their loss to Ireland is cause for weeping indeed. That the people of the north should be repeating the error is sad. "Put not your trust in Princes", says Psalms 146.3. But they all did.

England on a Clear Day

WE KNOW more about the English than they know about us. This is partly because the conquered one, the servant, the retainer, nearly always does know more about his lord and master than that superior and largely indifferent being knows about him. It is also because the Irish, like the other peoples on the Celtic fringe, the Welsh and the Scots, are on the whole better educated, class for class and person for person, than the English are. They have the same passion for education in general: and they have, as all the world knows, a particular passion for history. Probably the have-nots always think more about history than the haves; it is, after all, in the interests of possessing classes and peoples to forget about history, which is largely a record of how possessions were acquired; and consequently they are inclined to pretend that it did not happen, or that it was about ideas and noble abstractions and not about conquest and seizure and dispossession.

Anyway the Irish do think and care a lot about history. Even our daily newspapers are, somewhat to the amazement of visitors, full of discussions of historical cause and effect; political parties are rooted in particular and often conflicting interpretations of historical crises and developments; and though the debate about history has never ceased in the present writer's lifetime at least, it has of course taken on a new acerbity and a new complexity since the eruption of — to use the easy locution — 'the Northern troubles'.

But it is impossible to know anything at all about Irish history without also knowing a great deal about the English: about Henry VIII and the English Reformation, about Elizabeth and the Spanish threat, about Cromwell and Pitt and Gladstone. An Englishman could pass for someone who knew a bit about his country's history while having only a very hazy idea about Charles Stewart Parnell. An Irishman who knew nothing about William Ewart Gladstone would be an ignoramus.

Quite large numbers of Englishmen feel a general sort of diffused sympathy for Ireland; some, as we know too well, have been smitten by what they consider to be the charm of the people or the country; and a few, like the first Erskine Childers, have become unassuageable supporters of the Irish cause. But not many have been impressed by what could be called the sum total of the Irish achievement in the way that large numbers of Irish men and women have been impressed by what they regard as the sum total of the English achievement.

Those English who have expressed admiration for Ireland in fairly recent times have been mostly of a literary bent, and what has impressed them has been what seemed a remarkable abundance of talent and high spirits, often brought to bear on English life or subjects, as by Sheridan, Shaw and Wilde. Even where our literature is concerned, though, few Englishmen have succeeded in identifying the comic Irish vision with its elements of human camaraderie as clearly as many Irishmen have succeeded in identifying the calm English vision with its elements of human hope. In expressing praise of Shakespeare, Wordsworth, Blake, Dickens and D.H. Lawrence, it seems natural to praise England and the English people; less natural in the case of Joyce or Beckett to praise Ireland and the Irish people.

Nor, leaving Irish literature in English aside, have other specifically Irish things — the fierce continuity of the Gaelic tradition, the proclaimed egalitarianism of the republican, for example — seemed as remarkable or as admirable to much proportionately large numbers of English people as certain specifically English things — the stability of institutions, the genius for compromise, the assumption of equality before the law, for instance — have seemed to large numbers of Irish people. And, apart from the fact that we know more about them than they do about us, and that there may even be more to admire — for England after all has had a history, and we have not — the reasons are not really very far to seek. From the language to the legal system many things English have been successfully transplanted to Ireland. From the form of parliamentary assembly with its two major parties downwards, many English models are working and can be seen to be working more or less successfully in the new environment. Some of these transplants were accomplished by force, others of them by fraud: no matter, accomplished they were; and to such an extent that a very real if largely subconscious and unexpressed feeling exists among very many people in Ireland that without the English connection Ireland would still be a somewhat backward and benighted place.

The common and simplistic view on the other side of the Channel is, I know, that the Irish are natively and stubbornly "anti-English." That a sort of anti-English feeling, some of it quite rationally and logically grounded in fact, exists, no-one would deny, although it waxes and wanes very much according to the circumstances of the moment; but it is also true that a much larger number of Irish people than are usually credited with it or would ever wish to articulate it, have somewhere in the backs of their minds, the idea that England is the source and the English connection the safeguard of civilisation in this island.

This attitude, it is important to stress, differs from those that used to be defined by the Irish word *shoneenism,* the attitudes that made obeisance to Dublin Castle and the pathetic values of the vice-regal court. It is, for one thing, less obviously connected with greed, personal advantage or mere snobbism; indeed where certain forms of promotion and personal advantage are concerned those who hold it may deem it somewhat politic to suppress it or conceal it. But the fact remains that many, many people in Southern Ireland feel, consciously or otherwise (the feeling takes of course much more obvious, cruder and more identifiable forms in the North) that without England there would be no habeas corpus and trial by jury, no safeguards for personal freedom and scarcely any law and order; that beyond the English connection all is jobbery, obscurantism, envy, narrow-mindedness and the love of rapine and slaughter for their own sakes.

And just as anti-English feeling has its rational and its rational-historical side, so has this sort of pro-English sentiment. Urban civilisation and certain developed forms of trade and commerce, manufactury and exploitation in Ireland were for many centuries dependent on keeping the native Irishry beyond the pale which had an actual physical existence. The native Irish legal system did not run to habeas corpus and trial by jury. Neither, it might be added, did it run to gaols, transportation, massive confiscations of territory and the naked exploitation of resources by private individuals for their own gain; but no matter. The circumstances of Irish history and the limited forms of pacification achieved in England's interest by English law, always gave a colour to the belief that the appeal to violence came from the Irish side. They still do; and, the conflict in the north-eastern corner of the island aside for the moment, even the cruel events of the civil war of 1922-23, an English-inspired quarrel over an English-dictated document, at once made it seem as if all the gloomy prognostications that had been made throughout the period of Home Rule agitation about the bloodshed that would follow a loosening of the English connection were amply justified.

Now much of this feeling has been handed down as a sort of heritage from one possessing class in Ireland to another: from the Cromwellian settler to the eighteenth century trader or manufacturer, from the landowner to the Catholic merchant who came into his own after the passing of the Emancipation act; but it also has an identifiable connection with trades and avocations. Lawyers, after all, like the law. Parliamentarians like parliament. And though there are of course nationalist judges and lawyers, and very few of our southern parliamentarians would get elected if they did not make some sort of obeisance to old nationalist gods and shibboleths, on the whole lawyers tend to be firm admirers of English legal precedents, while the tendency of our legislature and our legal draughtsmen to cling as closely as possible to existant English models, new or old, is notorious.

Which brings us to poets and literary men in general, who write the language of Shakespeare, John Dryden and Samuel Johnson: write it of course with varying degrees of sensitivity, awareness and knowledge of the English tradition, but write it all the same. If you believe with Theobald Matthew Wolfe Tone (as the present writer does) that "the connection between Ireland and England is the curse of the Irish nation" and, as a matter of intellectual if not emotional conviction that "our independence must be had at all hazards"; and if you yet rejoice in using the English language and inheriting your share of its glories, you are, at first blush anyway, in a somewhat ambiguous position. To the outside observer it would appear at first as if you ought to belong to that portion of the Irish people who believe that the English connection is really, in one way or another, the source of all sweetness and all light and therefore must be, in one way or another, at all costs preserved.

In the days of the present writer's mis-spent youth the question of being an Irish poet who used the English language as distinct from being an English one who did the same used to be the subject of endless, fruitless and really very woolly-minded, not to say dishonest, debate; and he got a shock recently when he opened an issue of the English magazine *Aquarius* to find that such a debate was still dragging its weary and disconsolate length along. The fact is, though, that it was a Scottish issue; and the pages had been thrown open to the Scots to thrash around in on the subject of "What it feels like to be a Scottish poet". He read it with amazement and a feeling of *déjà vu* and horror for the days of yore so strong as to be stifling (forbye there were some intelligent contributions). But when he asked himself why these fusty old debates were no longer conducted hereabouts, the only answer he could find was the degree of independence we have achieved as compared to the Scots.

This is partly a political, or, more specifically, an institutional matter. We have an apparatus of discussion, criticism and propagation which they do not have, an apparatus which, like all such nowadays, is partly dependent on the state. We have an amount of publishing which would have been inconceivable a few years ago. But it is also partly a matter of confidence. The enormous and more or less simultaneous acquisition of Joyce and Yeats as founding fathers of a modern literature means that we have a tradition of our own to work in. It would be wrong to say that this frees us from Matthew Arnold, Thomas Hardy and W.H. Auden, nor would it be a good thing if it did; for to a writer using the English language the presence in his consciousness (or his unconsciousness, if you prefer it that way) of the great masters of the English tongue is an important matter which he would be the poorer without.

What it does mean is that we can take them or leave them in a way which was once not possible, just as it was not possible for the American poets who preceded Whitman, poets like Longfellow, Whittier or even Edgar Allan Poe to take or leave their English models or forebears; It is true that almost from the beginning of Irish literature in English there was an attempt to establish a sort of independence both in idiom and subject. This led to the excesses of unnatural Hiberno-English known as "Kiltartan" as well as to a restriction of subject matter in favour of the primitive, the tradition-bound, the patriarchal and the archaic. In other words the writers concerned were Irish with malice aforethought, literary nationalists with a national and not just a human stock-in-trade. And from the time of the so-called Irish Revival, the Celtic twilight period on, there was an evident paradox in the situation: the English, starved of pastoral as their countryside disappeared, starved of the mythological, starved of the primitive in their mock-Tudor suburbs, responded with glee. Both parties were, in their way, happy.

Well, all that is now coming to an end I am glad to say. Though there are still lingering traces of the mentality which created it, the Irish Revival, with its implications of a literatureless past just escaped and an esoteric hinterland which had an appeal because of its mere strangeness is, thankfully, almost over. The Celtic twilight, or fog, is being dispersed. We are very nearly free from the picturesque, the romantic-rural, the nostalgic-archaic, the historical archaeological, the tribal subconscious as our only modes. And the truth is that we are free from these deliberately nationalist, and therefore, in a deep sense truly provincial modes which appealed to the early Yeats and to the later and less spontaneous O'Casey precisely because we have won for ourselves a greater degree of national independence and national self-confidence in the matter of literature. (There are those who don't know that yet, but no matter.)

And hopefully too that blissful state will sooner or later apply in politics. I have dwelt at greater length on what I believe to be a curious current of pro-English feeling in this country than I have on the much-better publicised degree of anti-English sentiment, though on the subject of the latter, one should be wary of confusing a practical desire to end a political connection with anything that could be called anti-English feeling. However, pro or anti feelings are both undesirable. They feed on each other and they hinder all sorts of natural development. There is good reason to look forward to the day when, free from either, we can at length come to terms with all things English if only because, with its advent, many Irish people will also be able to see things Irish in a clearer light.

Anthony Cronin
HERITAGE NOW
Irish Literature in the English Language

"Anthony Cronin's reading is wide, his insights astonishing, his whole book suggests that we may well be ready for a unitarian approach to the literature of Ireland in English."
Anthony Burgess

"This is a good book to have around. It's at once warm and intelligent in its approach. It has an extremely sensitive feel for the essential qualities of the Irish voice as expressed in literature ... The verve of the discussion, the vivid connections established, open the topics freshly to us." *Tom McIntyre*

"After years of persistent attempts to open up the closed shop of so-called Anglo-Irish literature, Anthony Cronin has flushed it out with an explosive device called *Heritage Now*." *Francis Stuart*

Anthony Cronin
The Life of Riley

"A comic triumph." *New York Times*

"I must honestly admit that I have laughed more at *The Life of Riley* ... than at any other book I have ever read." *Benedict Kiely, The Irish Times.*

"A splendidly comic imagination." *Times Literary Supplement.*

"As richly comic a novel as one could find." *Chicago Daily News.*

Published by Brandon Book Publishers, Cooleen, Dingle, Co. Kerry.